Olivetti Headquarters, Milton Keynes, 1971

▲▶ Architectural Design Profile

JAMES STIRLING

CONTENTS

The Pursuit of the Art of Architecture, *Robert Maxwell*   5

THE ROYAL GOLD MEDAL, 1980
Introduction, *Norman Foster*   11
Acceptance, *James Stirling*   12
Concluding Address, *Mark Girouard*   19

THE PRITZKER PRIZE, 1981
The Pritzker Prize in Architecture   20
Pritzker Prize Acceptance, *James Stirling*   21

BUILDINGS AND PROJECTS
Complete List of Buildings and Projects   22
Selected Work 1950-1980   23
Dresdner Bank, Marburg 1977   40
Bayer AG PF Zentrum, Monheim, 1978   42
Staatsgalerie New Building and Chamber Theatre,
Stuttgart, 1977-83   48
    A Note to the Drawings, *Charles Jencks*   50
    Richtfest: Topping Out Ceremony, 1982   56
Luxury Houses, Manhattan, 1978   60
Science Centre, Berlin, 1979   64
Rice University, Houston, 1979   74
    Buildings in Context, *Paul Goldberger*   80
Fogg Art Museum New Building, Harvard, 1979-84   82
    A Style Crystallised, *Ada Louise Huxtable*   88
The Clore Gallery, London, 1980   90
    Literal Eclecticism, *Charles Jencks*   92
Acknowledgements   104

This survey of James Stirling's architectural work selected by the architect is published on the occasion of his receipt of two of architecture's premier awards, the Royal Gold Medal for Architecture 1980, and the Pritzker Architecture Prize 1981.

In the United Kingdom, the Royal Gold Medal for Architecture has been bestowed on architects of international stature since the year 1848. The Gold Medal for 1980 was presented to James Stirling at the Royal Institute of British Architects on 24 June 1980.

The Pritzker Prize has been established in the United States of America as architecture's Nobel Prize. The award to James Stirling was announced in New York on 15 April 1981. The presentation followed on 29 May 1981, at the National Building Museum in Washington DC.

The introduction by Norman Foster, James Stirling's response and the concluding address of Mark Girouard on the occasion of the award ceremony of the Gold Medal are reproduced here in full, together with the Commendation and James Stirling's speech of acceptance of the Pritzker Prize. In addition there are critical contributions by Robert Maxwell, Charles Jencks, Paul Goldberger and Ada Louise Huxtable.

This Profile was designed by Dennis Crompton with the cover drawing prepared for *AD* by James Stirling.

Academy Editions/St. Martin's Press

Olivetti Headquarters, Milton Keynes, 1971

Copyright © 1982 Architectural Design.

All rights reserved.

First published in Great Britain in 1982 in volume form
by Academy Editions, 7 Holland Street, London W8.

First published in the United States of America in
1982 by St. Martin's Press.

Library of Congress Catalogue Card Number
81-23245.

ISBN 0-312-43987-3.

Printed in Great Britain by Balding + Mansell Limited

The Pursuit of the Art of Architecture

Robert Maxwell

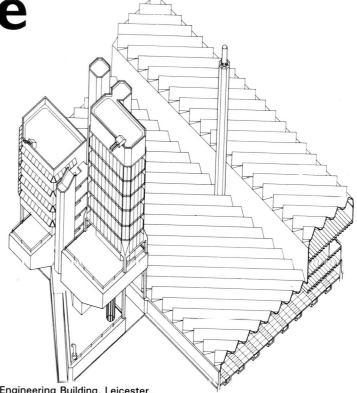

Engineering Building, Leicester,
James Stirling and James Gowan, 1959

It is gratifying, in retrospect, that James Stirling was awarded the RIBA Gold Medal no later than last year - so at least preceding his collection of the Pritzker Prize in 1981. If the order of giving had been reversed, it would have looked as if we were struggling belatedly to recognise merit where others had long discerned it. The prophet is not after all without honour in his own country.

And yet, within Britain, while Stirling is dimly understood to be out of the ordinary, he is hardly accepted as *great*. Hellman's comment on the Gold Medal Award showed a heavyweight figure skating over thin ice. Skating - here equated with artistic endeavour - is inappropriate both to the character of the architect as a burly type and to the deceptive nature of the environment as a source of joy, or whatever.

In England, in particular, there is a peculiar breath of scandal attaching to the pursuit of architecture as art. Criticism of architecture in the public mind is broadly associated with sociological or material failure, and these spectres haunt the practice of architecture. Yet when such faults occur - and they are commonplace in Booker's book - they are not thought to be really scandalous except when associated with high architectural aspirations. Aiming high, which must mean being concerned about

---

James Stirling has been the Wunderkind of modern architecture for some twenty years. Today he is a mature leader of world architecture.

Philip Johnson

---

something other than the mere avoidance of sociological or material failure, becomes itself the measure of an increased risk. To practise architecture as an art implies an idea of *hubris.* On the whole we feel safer if architectural aspirations are confined to the notion of building as a craft, using only well-tried methods corresponding to subservience to the social order. Even that approach, if followed closely, would probably appear as too radical in our consumer-oriented society, with its emphasis on good taste, usually degenerating into high-minded good taste. Stirling has repudiated such a limited role and has seen the need to actively avoid good taste. It was Stirling who said: 'Let's face it, William Morris was a Swede!'[1]

The risks which Stirling has been seen to take are paradoxically of two kinds, corresponding to two major phases of his career: at the beginning he was thought to be manipulating form in the name of modernity and then, when that was finally accepted, he suddenly appeared to be manipulating it in the name of history.

He came to public notice with the Stirling and Gowan masterpiece at Leicester University, in an uncompromisingly modern style which made no concessions to campus conformity but did however express the forthright stance of engineering research. The general stylistic language of non-conformity had been anticipated in the firm's design for Selwyn College (in 1959) and was followed by Stirling's own development in buildings for

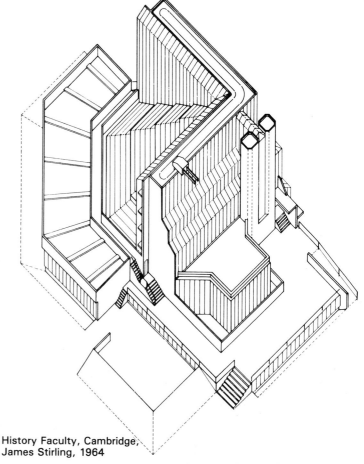

History Faculty, Cambridge,
James Stirling, 1964

Olivetti Training School, Haslemere, James Stirling, 1969

the universities of Cambridge (1964), St. Andrews (1964) and Oxford (1966).

The character of these buildings is in different degrees a celebration of modernity. They are all strictly within a canon of form following function, and they all show evidence of technological innovation, as in the use of adhesive red tiles to match with brickwork as a cladding skin, the use of greenhouse glazing in large areas, or the development of large-scale pre-cast structural units. They all fall within a concept of a modernity which, as in the orthodox view of Pevsner, was expected to display 'new methods and materials, the vital aspect of progressive architecture'.[2] In this spirit, too, the rounded plastic casings of the Olivetti Training Centre at Haslemere are an architectural equivalent of the modernity of industrial design for which Olivetti typewriters were famous.

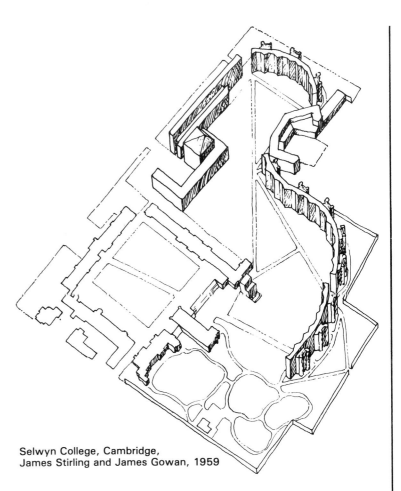

Selwyn College, Cambridge,
James Stirling and James Gowan, 1959

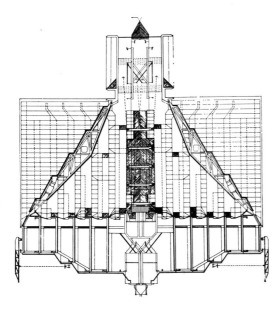

...discerning architects will discover evidence of James Stirling's continuing research into the celebrated occasions of our time.

Alvin Boyarsky

The search for technological innovation was obligatory both as an index of modernity and as a mark of continuity in the tradition of modernity, since it was technological innovation which identified the new spirit in the first place, in its most British beginnings. It is clear that Stirling identified himself with that tradition, both in its Britishness, and in its inventive enterprise, preceding as it did the subsequent aestheticising transformation of it in *L'Esprit nouveau*. 'One only has to compare the Crystal Palace with the Festival of Britain, or the Victorian railway stations with recent airport terminals, to appreciate the desperate situation of our technological inventiveness in comparison with the supreme position which we held in the last century.'[3]

Reyner Banham, in assessing the History Faculty at Cambridge, thought that it made all other recent buildings in Cambridge look effete. There is a tough-mindedness, a robust self-reliance, not only in its use of materials and in its technological directness, but also in the derivation and organisation of its forms and spaces, which place it in a heroic tradition of being modern. It entirely escapes the stigma of merely looking modern, it does not merely reproduce the 'modern' look, tied so often at this period to the excessive use of concrete or the image of Mediterranean cells. If anything, it looks British. But in terms of popular image it fulfils the Russian formalist prescription for art: it makes the familiar strange. It has to be learned to be loved.

In the seventies, new tendencies began to appear in Stirling's work: a new interest in context, in symmetry, in historical allusion. For those who had learned to love the tough-minded analysis of his heroic style, with its aura of an entirely native tradition of modernity, these new tendencies seemed to imply a *volte-face*. They certainly imply a revaluation of architecture as an ancient art embodied in an essentially European tradition. Neoclassicism is not an English invention even though England has in the past contributed its share to that development. Leon Krier, a good European, was possibly a catalyst, but the tendencies were there before his advent (Runcorn, designed in 1967, shows as much Neoclassicism as Siemens two years later), and indeed go back as far as the Isle of Wight house of 1956, which perhaps reflects the Neo-Palladianism of that moment.

Do these new tendencies really imply a *volte-face*? Stirling has been at pains to stress the continuity between his phases. His early work, of more domestic scale and character, was nearly all designed within a simple discipline of brick construction, but it also drew explicitly upon vernacular elements and the native functional tradition of barns and warehouses, as much as upon ideas of high modernity. His initial empiricism had a sound basis both in terms of

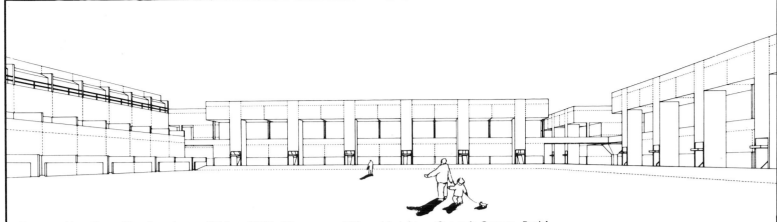

Runcorn New Town Housing, James Stirling, 1967, *'the same width and height as Queen's Square, Bath'*

overall economy and in terms of his own wish to acquire the rudiments of a constructional technique. Many aspects of early Stirling and Gowan have been absorbed into local authority housing conventions, and their familiarity today obscures the fact that they constituted a novel approach to the definition of a practical modernity which would be suitable for the British climate. Nowhere are there the signs of an international style, and indeed Stirling frequently inveighed against 'shoe box architecture' which

---

Humanistic considerations must remain the primary logic from which design evolves.

James Stirling

Queen's Square from the east side, T Maldon the younger, 1784

Martello Tower, late 18th century

as he correctly noticed was all too vulnerable to the mono-dimensional men, the developers who employed accountants. From the beginning, therefore, we must be aware in Stirling of a strong independence, and a depth of reflection on the nature of building and on the relation of building to expression. Single-minded his architecture has been, but never simple-minded.

He has also been at pains to point out — as distinct from the 'arbitrary' interpretations of critics (such as Jencks' insistence on the marine metaphor in St. Andrews) — the regular and architectonic sources of design ideas in his work.[4] These constitute a very wide collection of concepts and precedents ranging from sectioned machines (Sheffield) and Cotswold barns (Woolton House) to stately gate towers (Florey) and Inca

Siemens AG, Munich, James Stirling, 1969

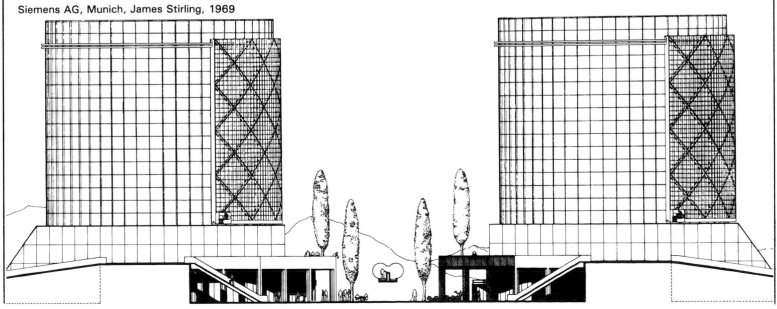

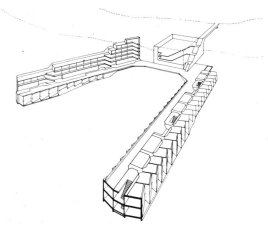

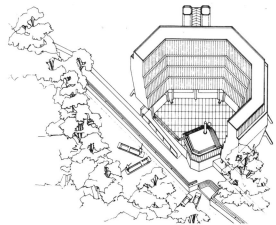

Residential Expansion, St. Andrews, James Stirling, 1964

Florey, Queen's College, Oxford, James Stirling, 1966

stonework (St. Andrews). The wide ranging source of his ideas is the mark of an extremely intelligent and even erudite sensibility, and shows that Stirling has always appreciated that form does not derive from function in a narrow sense, but only through the mediation of a tradition, that is within a cultural envelope.

Agreed that his architecture shows a consistency in its very depth of cultural relativity, it is still evident that a marked change of attitude has taken place since the beginning of the seventies, and that modernity in its first sense is no longer the sole aim of his work today.

It is tempting to consider again his debt to Le Corbusier. Stirling's own work shows an awareness of all the great men in the heroic age, including Kahn, and he has learned from all of them. But there is evidence that he has paid particular attention to both Wright and Le Corbusier, and in some ways wanted to reconcile their qualities in his own work. Aside from their work in its detail, both of these men had careers marked by abrupt changes of style. Corbusier's career has had a particular importance.

Stirling's main contributions to architectural criticism are contained in the two articles he produced in the mid-fifties, and these are both concerned with Le Corbusier's *volte-face*.[5] With Jaoul and with Ronchamp there appeared to be an abandonment of a rational, technologically progressive modernity for an emotional, technologically regressive vernacularity. Le Corbusier's change of heart, his acceptance of Algerian standards of workmanship, posed a problem and at the same time opened a door. Stirling meditated deeply the consequences of Corbusier having gone 'soft' with Ronchamp. Out of this meditation came a brick architecture which was not soft, but hard, hard with its precision of profile and in its ability to define abstract planes; empirical, but modern.

Stirling had always appreciated that Le Corbusier was an eclectic borrower, noting his debt to Mediterranean vernacular and his sensitivity to Indian forms. But in the very source of Stirling's style there was a problematic: modernity was never more to be a simple matter of only following function: it involved a necessary meditation on form, and on what I have called the two faces of form: the face that beckons on, and the face that looks back.

In a somewhat obvious way Corbusier's *volte-face* with Jaoul provided Stirling with a source of empirical freedom. It legitimated the flats at Ham Common and the subsequent explorations of a brick vernacular. It was the mastery of brickwork which permitted the greater adventurousness of the later university buildings. The modernity which was sought within the tough discipline of brick cross-walls was then released when larger commissions permitted a freer approach, including the vital element of technological innovation. But what was learned during those largely preparatory years was more than a constructional understanding of brickwork. It was rather a matter of how to extract from a recalcitrant material the immaterial and abstract qualities of a weightless architecture, of an architecture formed in the mind. Form, and its manipulation, becomes the source of infinite possibilities.

Peter Eisenman in his analysis of the Leicester Building is able to demonstrate rather convincingly that constructional elements

such as brick and glass are consistently played with as elements in a game of ambiguity and reversal.[6] This sophistication of conception (which it needed an American critic to discover) indicates that Stirling has deeply meditated the question of architecture as expression of its own articulations, that is, as language, confronted within all the problems of defining the language spoken in the act of speaking it. In the words of Manfredo Tafuri, 'Stirling has "rewritten" the "words" of modern architecture, building a true "archeology of the present".'[7]

His latest buildings have moved on to a kind of stripped Classicism halfway between Ledoux and outer space.

Ada Louise Huxtable

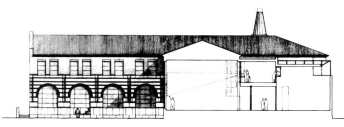

Architecture School Extension, Rice
James Stirling and Michael Wilford, 1979

There is no 'betrayal' of modernity in this, as some would have us believe, because 'modern' itself has been exposed as a kind of illusion, as a concept which dissolves the moment it is taken into meditation. There is a new kind of search for the locus of modernity in a non-utopian future. The appearance in Stirling's work of motifs which look back as well as look forward, of motifs carrying an extrinsic meaning, are a necessary consequence of this new area of search. They do not prevent, if they make more difficult, the parallel search for intrinsic meaning, for meaning, that is, which stems from the building as a mediated act of construction, as an artefact with its own rules of articulation, as an act of language and of the destruction of trite meanings.

I see us going forward oscillating, as I did as a student, between the formal and the informal, between the restrained and the exuberant.

James Stirling

The re-conversion of a vernacular of brick and glass into a high architecture of modernity had already ensured, by the end of the sixties, a place for Stirling at the international table, where he will shortly receive a dinner, a cheque and a Henry Moore. One suspects however that it is his second scandal, the scandal of

Villa Garches, Le Corbusier, 1927

Maison Jaoul, Le Corbusier, 1953

Ronchamp, Le Corbusier, 1950-55

historicity, which has supplied the element of notoriety and danger which seems to attach to him at present. In this he has moved faster than many younger architects to define where the action is. During the seventies events also have moved fast and the concept of modernity as the inalienable property of the Modern Movement in architecture has changed inexorably. Modernity today is the problem, in many ways more demanding, of rediscovering a 'now' within history, and within tradition.

Corbusier's 'going soft' with Ronchamp, his transformation of the rigid international style into a fluid and potent material for the exploration of his own sensibility, was a crucial influence on Stirling. It allowed him to develop his own, British, search for modernity. And when that had been achieved it still offered him the model, the provocation, for his further transformation into a grand master of the game.

But of what game?

In spite of the range of his reference, the subtlety of his allusions, the versatility of his models, Stirling's game is not a manipulation of our responses, but a meditation on his own. It is not an arbitrary accumulation of images, or a play with surfaces. It is wilful, perhaps but also full of determination and discipline. It comprises syntactic as well as semantic dimensions; and the balance of these, within the artefact, conveys an inner coherence - the sense of a convergence, however oblique, to a new and unexpected whole. In this he exemplifies what Robert Venturi has asserted to be the goal of artistic endeavour in architecture: 'the duty towards the difficult whole'.

Yet this whole is not ideologically remote or inaccessible. It is not in the first place an enigma to be unravelled only by the discerning scholar, although there will be much that only the discerning will see. It can be more simply read as the combined satisfaction of physical and psychological requirements, the extension of function towards ritual and of ritual towards the spareness and bleakness symptomatic of our age. No longer utopian, in a futuristic sense, it still deals with the reduction of values to essentials - not to essences but to relations. In this

Ben and Mary Stirling pictured in New York with J S shortly after hearing the news from Jay Pritzker

Stirling shows himself to be a modern, post-enlightenment, post-romantic, post-Darwinian, post-Einsteinian: the heir to a twentieth-century philosophy. As a modern he will search for truth in the fundamental patterns of life, neither refusing the past nor trying to retrieve a lost glory, but enjoying the vantage point of his own moment and his own sensibility, which is in that moment's potential. In this he exemplifies Le Corbusier's dialectic of head and heart, reason and passion, as he works between past and future, between what is known and what remains to be discovered.

His stance is thus essentially constructive, and his game is a game of discovery. His expression combines semantic, syntactic and pragmatic dimensions: the three essentials in Charles Morris' definition of language. What he discovers, is communicated, adds to our resources. In Stirling's language of expression we find figuration combined with abstraction, as we do in painting today, showing how closely he locates in the spirit of our time.

Stirling has not 'descended' into historical allusionism. He has brought to maturity and made self-evident his long-standing search for architecturality, for the essential ingredient, or rather mode of being, which makes architecture into more than mere utility. His search is important for the world because it demonstrates that modernity continues, that it has the scope and the duty to develop, although now prisoned within history, within tradition, within non-utopia. In spite of the apparent paradox, his own comments on the utopian aspects of Garches may justly be applied to the new modernity implicit in Stirling's work, the modernity which revives the possibility of the monument. For, according to Stirling, Garches was *a monument, not to an age which is dead, but to a way of life which has not generally arrived, and a continuous reminder of the quality to which all architects must aspire if modern architecture is to retain its vitality.*[8]

Notes

1 James Stirling, quoted in Paolo Portoghesi *Dopo L'Architettura Moderna*, 1980 p.194.

2 The phrase is taken from the sentence: 'An American middle-income family can afford a house built by new methods and materials, the vital aspect of progressive architecture'. James Stirling 'Regionalism and Modern Architecture' in *Architect's Year Book*, ed. Dannatt, 1957.

3 'Regionalism and Modern Architecture', op.cit.

4 His lecture at the Iran Conference of 1974, reported as 'Stirling Connexions' in *Architectural Review*, May 1975.

5 'From Garches to Jaoul', *Architectural Review*, Sept 1955; 'Ronchamp - Le Corbusier's Chapel and the Crisis of Rationalism', *Architectural Review*, March 1956.

6 Peter Eisenman, 'Real and English', *Oppositions* 4, Oct 1974.

7 Manfredo Tafuri, 'L'architecture dans le boudoir' in *Oppositions* 3, May 1974.

8 James Stirling, 'From Garches to Jaoul', op.cit.

At the time of writing this essay Robert Maxwell was Professor at the Bartlett School of Architecture, University College, London. He has now been appointed Dean of Architectural Studies, Princeton University, USA.

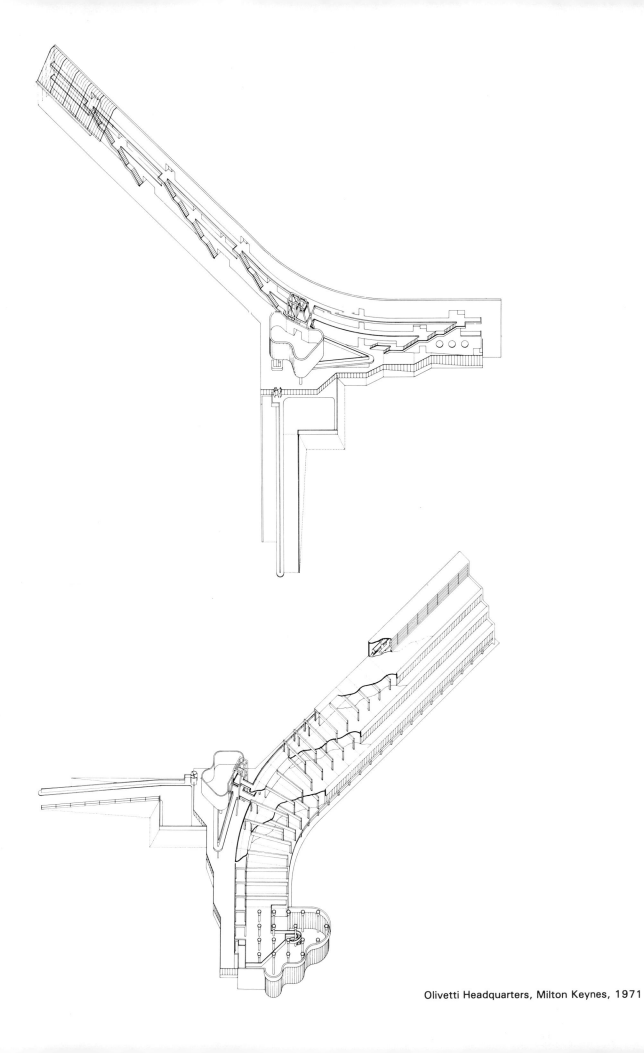

Olivetti Headquarters, Milton Keynes, 1971

Introduction to the Royal Gold Medallist

NORMAN FOSTER

President, Ladies and Gentlemen, we're here this evening to celebrate something that really happened a number of years back. A number of years back for many architects and students. Not only in the United Kingdom, but very significantly in Europe, the United States and as far afield as Japan. Namely, the recognition of James Stirling as an architect extraordinary.

By tradition the Gold Medal is awarded well after such reputations have become firmly established, and in comparison with previous years, Jim is a comparatively youthful recipient at fifty four. The name of Stirling has become an architectural byeword, but it has also been one of this country's invisible architectural exports in recent years, if not too much of a contradiction in words.

The list of limited competitions from Peru to North America to Germany is almost endless and in stark contrast with the leaner years here at home. Many influential drawings, in the absence of hard-edged commissions. It's still not without significance that he's currently working for three American universities and two German institutions.

In recent years the profession in this country has found itself increasingly under attack for its standards, quality and values. It does seem strange that during such a period, an architect of the calibre of Jim should be virtually dependent on recognition abroad. Their gain and our loss.

On this basis alone, he is now long overdue the kind of formalised recognition that the Royal Gold Medal stands for. Jim really brings together three forces; teacher, draughtsman and designer. All inextricably linked as James Stirling, the architect.

Regardless of workload, he's been a visiting Profesor at Yale for over twenty years now; and it was as a graduate student at Yale that I first came into contact with him. I recall that he was the kind of tutor who refused to say how he would do it, but rather force you back on your own resources by posing the awkward questions, and quite right too.

Much has been said about Jim's drawings; they seem to exist as abstracts in their own right and yet we know that they're design tools; a means to an end. Highly preferable in my view to current and unhealthy obsessions with architectural drawings as a kind of intellectual substitute for buildings. In the words of Charles Jencks, his drawings show the space, the structure, the geometry, function and detail, together without distortion. Or, as Reyner Banham notes, Stirling made the *all dimensions true* axonometric famous.

The drawings are, of course, inseparable from the buildings. Even if they appear as proof that the building has been considered three dimensionally from such diverse viewpoints as a mole with all-seeing eyes from below, or more likely from 45 degrees in a helicopter, hovering overhead. It's tempting to try to group the buildings in categories, and even more tempting to link them by quoting references from the architect or his critics.

The partnership with James Gowan, up to 1963, produced distinguished early works. Every one has its favourite, and for me the Leicester University Engineering Building around 1959 to '63 was a turning point. Although I enjoyed the earlier projects with their Corbusian roots, such as the Ham Common flats, Isle of White house and the Team Ten Village Infill. Each with their own overtones of a load-bearing brick vernacular. Leicester —

Leicester for me had a tension, an originality... and a drama which was born out of the everyday ingredients of materials and function.

The architect sets the nature of circulation and structure as generators provide insights. The appropriateness of hard, brittle and reflective surfaces to an outside climate; which virtually at the time created a new vocabulary for designers worldwide. A rediscovery of large-scale industrial glazing, of Victorian brickwork and tiles. Likewise a justification for the kind of cut and thrust of forces... of a column which seemed to penetrate a lecture hall in a totally arbitrary manner. This was described at the time by Jim in the following terms:

The weight of the towers above counter-balance the overhang of the lecture theatre under, or to say it another way, the extent of the cantilever of the lecture theatre is dictated by the amount of weight over. If you removed the top floor, the building would overturn. No doubt there is a certain architectural quality inherent in the composition of stable masses; particularly when they're asymmetrical.

It seems to me that there's a kind of recurring characteristic there, almost deliberately creating a difficult if not impossible design situation, which then has to be resolved. Which results in an enormous, kind of studied casualness; and I find this characteristic repeats itself in Jim's work: The apparently random disposition of elements in the Olivetti training school at Haslemere, for example. And I find this kind of studied casualness a very English characteristic, and it would be an interesting point to develop by working back in time and citing historical precedents. If Leicester belongs to that group of hard, brittle-skinned buildings in the same way as the Cambridge History Library and the Florey Building at Oxford, then there are also those projects where structure dominates, such as the unbuilt Dorman Long headquarters, incidentally a personal favourite. Through to those more sensuous extruded or moulded buildings, like St. Andrews, the housing at Runcorn or again the Olivetti building. The latter evocative of the company's own artifacts. And at the same time, quite interestingly, this pioneering thing. Pioneering in that sense, the application of more advanced materials, such as GRP.

And out of this background of building groups, which evolved in a kind of linear sequence, we come to the current projects with more manifest urban and historical associations, which I know Jim will be talking about later this evening.

I particularly like the way that he summed up in a talk in Bologna when he said, and I quote the end of that talk:
The structural content in architecture is likely to increase as traditional methods of construction decline, and new buildings get larger and more complicated. However, I think it will be ever more necessary for architects not to rely merely on the expression of techniques for the architectural solution. Humanistic considerations must remain the primary logic from which a design evolves.

And if I have to condense that, and I underline the last sentence, *humanistic considerations must remain the primary logic from which a design evolves*, that would be my own particular key extract.

It's my honour and delight to support James Stirling for the Royal Gold Medal in Architecture in 1980.

Thank you.

Acceptance of the Royal Gold Medal in Architecture 1980

JAMES STIRLING

There are many who have helped me and I must start with some thanks. Firstly, going back to the beginning — to my mother who was a Scottish/Irish schoolteacher and who early on perceived that I had no heart for my father's wish that I should follow him in going to sea — my father was the archetypal Scottish chief engineer. Ironically it was my discovery of his 'apprenticeship' drawings — beautiful blue and pink wash sectional drawings of machine parts, turbines, ships' engines, etc. that first opened my eyes to the elegance of functional draughtsmanship.

Later at architectural school I would thank my good friend and teacher *then* as *now* — Colin Rowe — I must have been one of the first of the many hundreds, perhaps thousands, of students he has turned on.

In London I would thank the architectural firm of Edward Lyons, Lawrence Israel and Tom Ellis (Lyons, Israel and Ellis) where I finally settled and learnt the conventions of job running, contracts, site visiting etc.

Then I would thank my first client — in particular Leonard Manusso — for whom we built the flats at Ham Common. He had great trust in encouraging me in 1956 to set up an office and start a practice.

I particularly wish to thank everyone who has worked with me, consultants, staff, associates and partners, partner at the beginning James Gowan and in the last several years Michael Wilford.

Then there are the patrons — almost all our work has come directly or indirectly from fellow architects, both in the UK and abroad, and I would especially mention Sir Leslie Martin who recommended us for several University projects and who also greatly helped many of my contemporaries.

I'm sorry not to have mentioned others to whom I am grateful — but time is short, and to move on.

I've always been a designer with wide ranging interests and perhaps eclectic tendencies; it could hardly have been otherwise, my architectural education was from the books. As a young man I did not work in an office or through the English system of being an articled pupil — a practice which seemed to be dying out (about 1945) just as I went to architecture school — so my problem was not one of working for a master, or of getting out from under the influence of one.

Rather, at Liverpool under Professor Budden, to succeed, one had to be good in many styles. In first year we did renderings of classical orders followed by the design of an antique fountain, and at the end of that year we had to design a house in the manner of C A Vosey — quite a span of history.

In the following years we oscillated backwards and forwards between the antique and the just arrived 'Modern Movement' — which for me was the foreign version *only*, — as taught by Colin Rowe. In addition to *Towards a New Architecture*, the book which influenced me most at this time was Saxl and Wittkower's huge atlas-like *British Art and the Mediterranean*, this much more so than Wittkower's later *Architectural Principles.* This large book was the one that none of us students could ever get to fit onto our plate glass and wire, Albini style bookshelves, it just lay around on the floor and got looked at.

With such an education I developed obsessions through the entire history of architecture — a situation which is still with me — though at certain times I'm more interested in some particular aspects than others.

Regarding some of those aspects — somewhere in the middle years at Architecture School I had a passion for 'stiff' art nouveau designers like Mackintosh and Hoffman, less so for their English equivalents such as Voysey and Baillie Scott. This interest was supplanted towards the final year by Le Corbusier and the Italian rationalists.

As soon as I graduated and got to London in 1950, I set about visiting the bombed out churches of Hawksmoor. I was intrigued by English baroque architects such as Archer, Vanburgh and Hawksmoor and admired the ad-hoc technique which allowed them to design with elements of Roman, French and Gothic etc. — sometimes in the same building.

Also during those early years in London I learned about the Russian Constructivists — about whom I knew nothing when studying in Liverpool — there were just no books on them, though they did have the book on Asplund which I devoured, perhaps I should say acquired. However, my fascination with the Modern Movement never really got more recent than early Corb and the Constructivists, and in the early 50s I developed an interest in all things vernacular from the very small — farms, barns and village housing to the very large — warehouses, industrial buildings, engineering structures, including the great railway sheds and exhibition sheds.

Somewhere in the mid 50s (was it to do with finding a *genuine* brutalism?) I became interested in the stripey brick and tile Victorian architects — like Butterfield, Street, Scott, etc. and when I went to the US as a visiting critic I found the asymmetric 'turn of the century' timber shingle houses of even a town like New Haven an eye opener and more interesting than Saarinen or SOM — the current heroes. Though I do confess I was impressed by a limited period of Frank Lloyd Wright's production — particularly the concrete block houses around Los Angeles. During my first visits to the US I was also aware of the incredibly high finish and *way out* aspect of New York art deco buildings — such as the Chrysler tower among others. In the whole of Europe it seemed to me we had nothing to come near to them.

Factory, West London

The reading room, British Museum

Trinity College, Cambridge, 1500

I'd known the Soane Museum from the early 60s and later I became interested in Neoclassical architects like Soane, Gandy, Playfair, Goodridge. Their German counterparts, Gilly, Weinbrenner, Von Klenze, Schinkel seem to me to extend the process into a later date with a far greater juxtaposition of scales and materials. Actually it is the transition from Neoclassical into Romantic style in the first half of the 19th century which I find particularly interesting — the move from that abstract, sparse, Neo-classicism which somehow carried a maximum of emotive association   to the break up of Classicism with the incoming language of realism and naturalism — a fascinating circumstance which I think has parallels in the architectural situation today.

I do not have time to go further. If I could I would surely refer to English castles and French chateaux, to Bavarian roccoco and Italian gardens, to Venetian palazzos and English country houses, and more. But now I should switch to our own limited production.

We are alas too well known for a small part of our output, namely the University buildings of the early 60s particularly at Leicester and Cambridge and recently I've heard the comment 'Why has our work changed so much?'. Whilst I think change is healthy, I do not believe that our work has changed. Maybe what we do now is more like our earlier work, and that oscillating process is still continuing.

The Leicester, Cambridge, Oxford projects have been referred to as expressionist, or constructivist and even futurist and, whilst this may be so, they also have more humble origins, — such as Leicester's backward look to the typical pre-war industrial estate factory where the office block is up front and the workship behind. And Cambridge's reference to 19th century public reading rooms with glass lantern roofs. Whilst the Oxford building tries hard to make connections to the courtyards of the Oxbridge College.

I think our projects have tended to come in series. Brick buildings in the 50s, glass skin and tile buildings in the early 60s. Then there were buildings in precast concrete and in the later 60s 'high-tech', so-called, buildings of prefabricated plastic. Then in the 70s there is the attempt to incorporate the more familiar appearance of public buildings in stone and render.

In 1971 we had the problem of designing in an historic/preservationist context — in the centre of old St. Andrews. We had to plan a gallery and studios alongside an 18th century house by taking down adjoining properties and at the same time, preserving the entrance lodges. With the forecourt solution, we proposed a new outdoor room for the town — a transitional space between Town and Gown.

In 1975 we were invited to take part in two limited competitions in Germany — both in historic centres and both

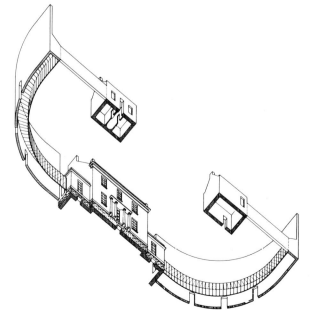

Arts Centre, St. Andrews University, 1971

The Graberplatz, Düsseldorf

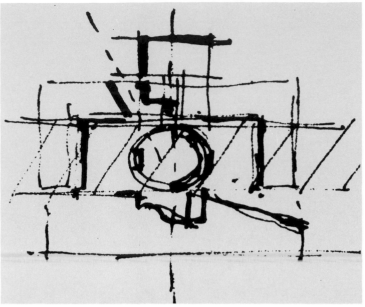

Sketch, New State Gallery, Stuttgart, 1977

Museums. In Germany many public buildings go to competition and recently there has been a tendency to invite in foreigners — maybe some local politicians consider that German architecture is well built but perhaps lacking in imagination. At Düsseldorf there was a concern to preserve existing buildings and facades, so we buried the new building in the centre of the city block — but pulled out an entrance pavilion, as it were, to represent and symbolise the whole museum. It also marks the start of the mandatory public footway, crossing the site — these short cut footpaths are a *democratic* requirement in many German competitions though I'm not convinced that it's in the best interest of urban centres as it tends to weaken the city block as an entity.

At Cologne (the second competition) the massing of new buildings either side of the Hohenzollern Bridge reinforces the axes of the railway crossing the Rhine on the axis of the Cathedral. The Museum is at its bulkiest farthest from the Cathedral and the ecclesiastical aspect of the entrance hall and other parts is also in deference to the Cathedral.

The next Geman competition in 1977 for the extension of the State Gallery and Theatre at Stuttgart we did win — it's now well on its way up. The old gallery is Neoclassical and U-shaped in plan. There is a semi-circular drive to the entrace and the mid point of the forecourt was marked by a classical urn — later replaced by a man on a horse. Stuttgart was bombed out and even more destroyed by the reconstruction — so preservation of existing buildings was an important requirement of the competition. The new building is also U-shaped in plan, but instead of a man on a horse it has a taxi drop off pavilion; instead of a semi-circular forecourt it has a circular garden. The wing of the experimental theatre balances the wing of the existing gallery. Referring to some notes from our report that went in with the competition:

SITE LAYOUT AND TOWN PLANNING, OBJECTIVES

1 "To bring the public moving diagonally on a new footpath into meaningful contact with the building (again the requirement for a footpath across the building site). This footpath passes at high level around a circular court then down to the entrance terrace — and through the arch under the new Theatre to the corner of the Eugenstrasse. It is hoped this routing will stimulate people to visit the gallery."

The new building may be a collage of old and new elements, Egyptian cornices and Romanesque windows but also Constuctivist canopies, ramps and flowing forms — a union of elements from the past and present. We are trying to evoke an association with museum and I find examples from the 19th century more convincing than examples from the 20th.

2 "To continue a three metre high terrace with car parking along

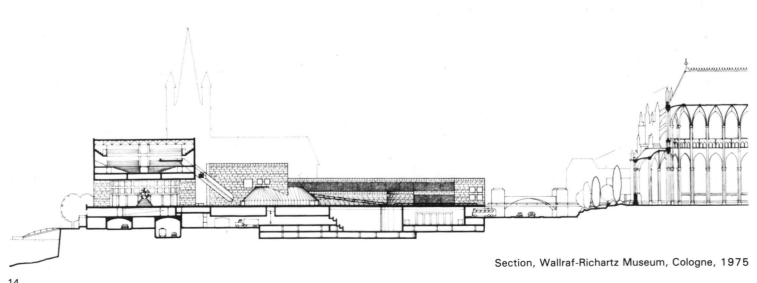

Section, Wallraf-Richartz Museum, Cologne, 1975

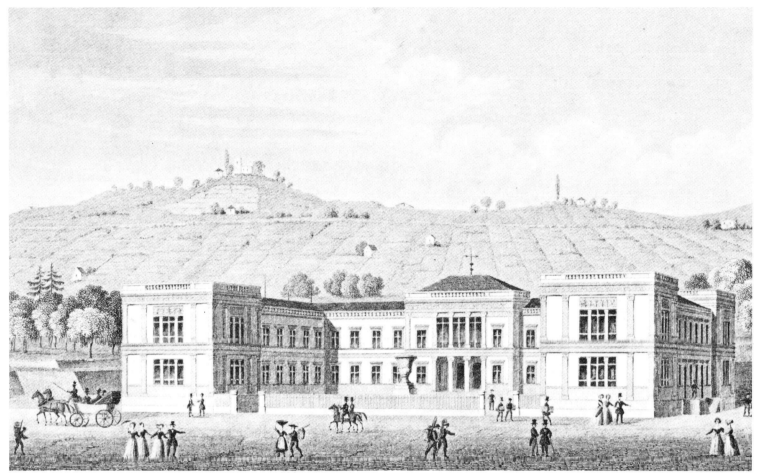

The existing Stuttgart gallery, *Gottlieb Georg Barth,* 1838
Dulwich Art Gallery, *John Soane,* 1814

Schloss Solitude

Konrad Adenauerstrasse and allow the possibility for a footbridge across Eugenstrasse. Directly off this terrace are the public entrances to the Gallery and Theatre.''

3 "By design of the new buildings, respect the axial/frontalising characteristics of the existing State Gallery and State Theatre and by siting of the new theatre wing allow the possibility for a public plaza on Eugenstrasse to develop." The theatre wing is set back from the street and we showed in the competition how a similar set-back could be made across the street when the adjoining site was developed. In this way a new public plaza on the axis of the existing State Theatre could be planned.

4 "To reinforce the traditional relationship of buildings to street — by retaining *all* existing buildings on Urbanstrasse and Eugenstrasse thus maintaining the street character of this area."

Regarding the galleries:

OBJECTIVES

1 "To create a sequence of well proportioned Gallery rooms, avoiding endless flexible space or gymnasic roof sections."

2 "To allow the public to flow without physical or psychological break between the new and old buildings — hence no change in floor level or awareness of crossing a bridge."

3 "The Administration offices are located in the upper levels of the building facing Urbanstrasse into which there is a separate non-public staff entrance."

There is a hierarchy in the entrance canopies — three modules over the gallery entrance, two over the theatre entrance and one over the staff entrance. Also with windows; i.e. over the staff entrance are small windows for the assistant Directors and above is a large window for the Director.

In 1978 we were asked to take part in another German competition — an Agro/Biochemical Research Centre for Bayer at Leverkusen. This was a site where there was no context — just an open flat field — so we had to invent a context.

SITE LAYOUT OBJECTIVES

1 "The Laboratory complexes and Administration building are sited with the intention of creating an idyllic Research Centre in an arcadian setting, with similar *buildings-to-landscape* relationships as achieved in the 18th century with the large country house (or German Schloss) and its attendant outbuildings set amid picturesque landscape."

2 "The Laboratory Complexes are positioned radially around a park and each is planned as a group of buildings around an internal garden. The buildings overlooking the park would be completed in the first construction phase and the 150% expansion requirement is provided by extending in an outward direction. The integration and identity of the Adminstration and Laboratories would be established at the outset and be preserved through all stages of expansion. Overall, we are attempting a visual alliance of sophisticated/technical aesthetic, with a vernacular/rusticated character. Staff and visitors using the lounges, arcaded corridors and internal gardens should feel what they are experiencing is more akin to a sequence of Florentine courtyards and gardens than the merely functional environment of an anonymous Research Centre."

3 ''The Administration offices are at the mid point — adjacent to the site entrance and contained in a U-shaped tower which, as a focal point, spatially counter-balances the radiating Laboratory Complexes. The Conference Centre is located at garden level in the base of this building.''

4 "From an Entrance Plaza there is access to the Administration building or down stepped ramps into the public park."

I am frequently accused by German architects of being fascist and monumentalist. The latter I do not mind as I consider it is an architect's responsibility — when appropriate — to design monuments and landmark buildings. For me a city without monuments is not a city. Small can be beautiful — and monumental — it is not a matter of size but rather a matter of *presence* — a chair can be monumental.

"This park is for the everyday use of staff and public. The ground is formed as a shallow bowl with groupings of specimen and exotic trees. The edge is defined by a canal with parallel lines of trees. Footbridges over lead into garden pavilions (gazebos) at the entrance of each Complex. Gates on these footbridges would restrain the public from wandering into the Laboratories."

5 "Circulation routes extend like spines down the length of each Complex, with subsidiary corridors serving Laboratory wings planned on three levels. There is an open services floor on the roof of each Laboratory stack." This project may appear extremely formal and that aspect a recent change in our work, but this is not so — our Churchill College project of the 1950s indicates that formal designs have always been part of our vocabulary, also from the 1950s our School Assembly Hall which is quite symmetrical, and from more recent times, the housing squares at Runcorn are both formal and symmetrical.

The next German competition in 1979 we did win, and it will be completed in 1984. This is for the upcoming 1985 Interbau where, instead of concentrating all the new buildings in a single area as previously, the idea this time is that they will be sited in different parts of Berlin — where each can be beneficial, even remedial, to an immediate area. This building is for the Bonn Government and is really a Think Tank — but called a Science Centre — an Institute for deep thinking on matters of ecology, environment, sociology, management etc. We also have to re-use the huge old Beaux Arts building (by the same architect who built the Reichstag) which somehow survived the war. Having destroyed so much with the post-war reconstruction they now want to hang onto everything which is old and remains. Reading again from the competition report:

OBJECTIVES

1 "The primary need is for a great multitude of small offices and a particular concern was how to find an architectural and environmental solution for a programme composed of repetitive offices. The *typical* office plan usually results in boring box-like buildings and the banality of these rationally produced offices may be the largest single factor contributing to the visual destruction of our cities in the post-war period."

So, I made an early decision that, whatever, we would break away from the office block stereotype, and I said to those working on it, *let's make a clustering of buildings — take for instance a long bar, a cruciform, a half circle and a square, and juggle them together with the old building.* Quoting again from the report: "Our proposal is to use the three Institutes of the Centre (Management, Social and Environment) plus the element for future expansion to create a grouping of buildings, all of which are similar, but different, and the architectural form may relate to familiar building types with each Institute having its own identifying building."

2 "Each Institute has two directors with complimentary staff and a binary organisation seems fundamental. As the buildings have symmetrical planning, allocation of rooms should adapt to this dual organisation rather well."

3 "The new buildings cluster around an informal garden with the single large tree at the centre preserved. The loggias and arcades which overlook the garden also relate to the cafeteria, the conference facilities and the old building. Free standing is the Library tower with a reading room at ground level."

We hope to make a friendly, unbureaucratic place — the opposite of an *institutional* environment — even accepting that the functional programme is for a repetition of offices in a single complex. Actually the whole can function as a single complex, as each building is joined at every level.

The irony is that whilst we have varied the building form we have retained an aspect of repetition in the wallpaper-like application of windows. A decision in regard to the typical office was that each would have a single centrally positioned window with flanking walls, for curtains, bookshelving etc.

External walls are rendered in putz with alternating colour — pink and grey per floor.

I have been asked to make some observations about working in Germany — though our building experience there is very limited. Firstly, I have been surprised to find that it is the established architects who are the architectural critics much more so than the

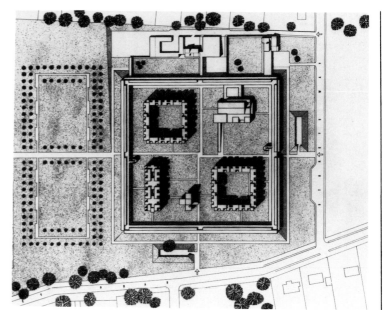

Churchill College, 1958

journalists or historians — the reverse of the situation here. We have been attacked by several well known architects, but at the same time we have had sympathetic, friendly and welcoming criticism from others. The professional critics seem to have a subdued role — maybe they are constrained by libel — whereas an established architect can say and print whatever he likes about another architect — and does.

Secondly, I am very impressed by the extremely high standard of building. Methods of insulation, thermal barriers, fixing of materials, acoustics etc. etc. are laid down and are absolutely mandatory and cannot be adjusted in relation to a budget. This is a relief as it removes any temptation to juggle the cost of technical details with the cost of architectural input, something which I have often found a problem here, particularly with low cost budgets which almost all our buildings have been (i.e. University Grants Commission).

Thirdly, it does seem that you should haggle over fees even though the percentages and ratings are set out in the documents. However, the documents do not refer to the continuous claiming process by which architects increase their entitlement and which seems normal practice. Unless you have been tipped off about this and other subtleties, you can catch a very bad cold indeed.

There has been no problem in setting up an office in Germany and maybe that is to do with the Common Market, though the bureaucracy seems even more rigid and inflexible than it is in the UK. Building sites appear incredibly clean and efficient, however building costs are more — maybe twice what they are here. Surprisingly, buildings do not seem to go up any faster — though, as I have said, they end up very well built.

In America our first project was for a developer who asked Richard Meier and ourselves to make separate schemes for luxury town housing on a street in the 'posh' upper east side of New York. He thought that each house should have its own lift, and his requirement was for eleven houses with maybe some apartments.

The whole was to be five storeys and built over an underground parking garage which had included in its roof structure — at ground level — a row of structural beams on eighteen foot centres to support the party walls of the houses to be built on top.

We used this beam spacing to plan an eighteen foot wide (thin man) house alternating with a thirty six foot wide (fat man) house, the latter on three lower floors with an independent apartment on the two upper floors. We were therefore able to plan three varieties of dwelling.

The movement backwards and forwards of the street facade expresses the house within the terrace and the application of bay windows, studio glazing, balconies etc. indicate the more important spaces within. This is similar to surface projections, windows, entrances etc., on traditional New York Townhouses and Brownstones.

These dwellings would be for sale in the luxury market and are planned with utmost dollar per square foot utilisation of floor area — there is no vertical space and planning is quite dense. The small front garden set behind railings is also similar to sidewalk and basement areas in this part of New York.

In 1979 we were commissioned by Rice University in Texas, Columbia University in New York and Harvard University for new buildings. Fortunately, due to finalising building accommodation, the phasing has slipped and we are able to design in sequence, not all at the same time. The new building for the Fogg Museum at Harvard is on the drawing boards and we are just starting with Columbia.

The last project is for extending the School of Architecture at Rice. The original campus by Cram, Goodhue and Ferguson is from the 1920s in a sort of Venetian, Florentine, Art Deco and we were asked to work within a limited range of bricks, pantiles, pitched roofs etc. — which is reasonable for this eccentric but elegant campus where there are many arcades, marble balconies and fancy spires.

The School of Architecture is an L-shaped building and we are extending it with another L-shaped piece. The interlock is joined by a surgical splint — a galleria or circulation core binding the two pieces together and connecting the old entrance with a new entrance at opposite ends of the splint. These entrance areas are lit through glass spires on the roof. The galleria overlooks a new exhibition space on one side and a jury room on the other.

The existing building is connected with a colonnade to an adjoining building and the L shaped extension creates a three sided courtyard — a sheltered garden in an otherwise very open campus.

It may be difficult to distinguish the facades of the new building from the existing ones, and for those who think this design is uncharacteristically quiet or conventional, I show a project from the 1950s (Mavrolean Houses) to indicate that the reserved and restrained — like the formalism of other projects — is not a change in our work. Both extremes have always existed in our vocabulary; so if we have a future, I see us going forward *oscillating*, as I did as a student — between the formal and the informal, between the restrained and the exuberant.

Thank you.

New York town house

Mavrolean Houses, 1957

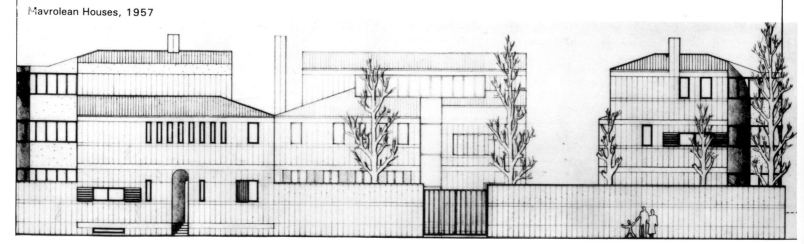

Royal Gold Medal Presentation Concluding Address

MARK GIROUARD

When I first had to write about Stirling's buildings, I went to see a good few of them and I thought about them and finally was very pleased with myself. Being a historian, I decided that Stirling was the Butterfield of modern architects. Then, a little later, I was talking to John Summerson and he said that he had been thinking about Stirling's buildings with great interest and had decided without any doubt that he was the Norman Shaw of modern English architecture. A little later, I met someone else, and I cannot quite remember who it was, and he told me that he was sure that Jim was the Hawksmoor of modern English architecture.

If there is a moral in this, it is that Jim is someone who is very interested in and reacts to old buildings but he is not an historian; he does not, I think, see himself as coming in some particular historical sequence. He reacts very strongly to all kinds of different buildings, ranging from warehouses to baroque palaces, but he reacts to them insofar as they relate to something which is going on at the time and he is prepared to adapt all sorts of different things and produce something which is quite unlike anything that has been produced before.

If one is looking for a name to attach to him or stream to put him in, certainly the very last I would like to use is that which tended to be used when I first started becoming aware of his buildings, and that was brutalist. I remember reading a reference, I think by Ian Nairn, in the *Buildings of England*, Surrey Volume, referring to his Ham Common flats saying, rather ambivalently, but saying *it would be nice to see a bloody minded style in England again*, and these Ham Common flats *were something that was on the way to this new bloodyminded style.*

There was a feeling in the air that here was **Big Jim**, this big man, somehow producing aggressive, extraordinary buildings that were sort of revolutionary; deliberately different and reacting and protesting and giving you terrific aesthetic shock that could be described by the word brutalist. Then I went out to Ham Common and was absolutely amazed. There I saw, what seemed to me, these exquisite, reticent, beautifully scaled, delicate, totally inoffensive, (in the nasty sense of the word), buildings which really were a pleasure and a delight to look at.

I started wondering, and here perhaps is a parallel with my Butterfield, there was a stage when people used to get fascinated by William Butterfield and what they called his *sadistic hatred of beauty*; and they got a kind of *frisson* from looking at Butterfield buildings. But now, the more one studies Butterfield, the more one realises that that was not the way he looked at his buildings at all. He was a very creative architect who could use buildings that were very unlike anything that had gone before. But in doing so there was no sadistic, shock impulse behind it. He describes his buildings in fact by words like gay and pretty, and when you look at something incredibly elegant, like All Saints, Margaret Street, that phrase *sadistic hate of beauty* does seem irrelevant. Yet I think that it did arouse this feeling because it was so unlike anything that had gone before.

I would really like to get away from trying to put Jim's buildings into a sort of art historical setting, and say what has given me personally the greatest pleasure. I would choose three characteristics. Shapeliness, delicacy and gaiety. Characteristics which are as far removed from brutalism as possible.

Shapeliness... after the war I think there was rather a feeling that if a building had a very strong shape, there must be something wrong with it. That terrible word formalist was bandied around. And yet it has always been to me one of the delights of both Jim's buildings and his exquisite drawings that they have this terrific quality of shapeliness. Whether they are actually symmetrical or whether they are asymmetrical, they always have this terrifically elegant shape; and it just is a pure pleasure to me to come across a building like the Leicester building or the Florey building or the History Faculty building in Cambridge and just walk round it and revel in this exquisite object.

Related to this is the quality of delicacy. One of the most likeable aspects of Jim's buildings is that when so many modern buildings are so very overbearing, his own buildings, though strange in some ways or unusual to people who are used to more conventional buildings, are always delicate in scale, never overpowering. He has a very strong feeling for the weave of a city. This is something which is becoming increasingly evident in his latest projects, when he has been given the chance which he did not have before, of putting buildings into an existing context. He has a very strong feeling for the really delicate scale of old cities and of old buildings. He is not going to produce great, overbearing buildings in which one feels that one is somehow being squashed or oppressed. He has this quality of delicacy — the buildings have some of the delicate character of a giraffe or gazelle.

It is sad, I think, that this quality of Jim's has been limited, on the whole, to academic projects, let alone to projects mainly outside this country. I feel awfully depressed that here is someone more interested, like Lutyens, in the spaces that one moves through, rather than the rooms that one ultimately ends up in. How sad it is that his scheme for Derby never got off the ground. That wonderful galleria would have been the most fantastic place. How sad it is that he still has not been given the opportunity of designing a great square or place in the centre of a big city. He, of all living architects, could produce a place in a city, a big square that would be a fantastic pleasure to walk in.

This brings me to the last quality of gaiety, which again is a quality which is all too desirable in large buildings in big cities and on the whole, all too lacking. I remember when my wife first saw the Florey building she burst into roars of laughter.

I told this to Jim and I am delighted to say that far from taking it as an insult, he expressed considerable pleasure. Quite rightly so, because it actually was a compliment; and it is all too rare now that modern buildings have this quality of entertaining one and giving one pleasure. It is something which is very present in Jim.

One of the qualities I always like about Jim's building, which is part of this element of gaiety is the element of colour. I was delighted to hear him reminiscing about his father's engineering drawings, and saying that they were coloured blue and pink. I somehow feel that an awful lot of modern architects today would have edited out that blue and pink in their minds, because blue and pink are not austere enough. But the colour of Jim's buildings is always a pleasure to me. The glowing red combined with the crystalline glass of his buildings of the 50s and 60s and now, in his buildings that are coming up, a combination of stripes in different brick or squares in different coloured stone and marble. This very strong element of colour.

I'm reminded of a phrase by Dr Johnson when the actor Garrick died. He said that his death had *eclipsed the gaiety of nations*. Well thank goodness Jim is not dead; he is with us we hope for many years to come, and I hope that the gold medal, rather than being, so to speak, a stone around his neck, will be a shot in his tank and that he will go on for many years to come to add to the gaiety and pleasure of nations. Thank you.

The Pritzker Prize in Architecture 1981

The Pritzker Prize is an international award established by the Hyatt Foundation in 1979 to honour the lifetime contributions of pre-eminent architects all over the world. In 1979 the Prize was given to America's Philip Johnson, and in 1980 to Luis Barragan of Mexico. Each received $100,000, and a cast of Henry Moore sculpture created specifically for the purpose.

The Prize was conceived during a conversation between the late King Gustavus VI Adolphus of Sweden and Carleton Smith, an advisor to many important philanthropic organisations. His Majesty pointed out the fact that Alfred Nobel, in setting out the guidelines for the Nobel Prizes in his will, had omitted many vital areas of human endeavour; the King felt that it would be appropriate to establish international prizes of similar magnitude for such disciplines as architecture and archaeology.

Smith took the idea to the Pritzkers, one of America's most prominent families whose business interests encompass publishing, real estate, electronics, timber, mining, and the Hyatt Hotel chain. Jay A. Pritzker set up the Hyatt Foundation to fund and administer the Pritzker Architecture Prize.

In establishing the Prize, Pritzker explained the rationale behind it: *By rewarding outstanding creative endeavours, we hope to further stimulate creativity and contribute to a deeper sensitivity. The award is being given annually to a living architect or architectural group whose work demonstrates a combination of talent, vision and commitment that has produced a consistent and significant contribution to humanity and the environment.*

To make certain the award truly reflects international architectural achievements, nominations are accepted from all nations and from architects, architectural societies, academicians, government officials, writers, critics, as well as leaders in related fields.

On awarding the prize to James Stirling in 1981, the Jury recorded their assessment of the quality of the architect's work in the following commendation:

James Stirling is still a relatively young man, and in honouring him we are looking both back at the remarkable achievement of his work to date, and forward to the realisation of new masterpieces. This is appropriate in paying tribute to an artist whose best work tempers an essentially modern approach with elements drawn from a deep appreciation for, and an extremely civilised relationship with the past.

Stirling's feel for the delicate weave of a complex of buildings has resulted in the creation of modern works which reverberate deeply and harmoniously with the traditional structures surrounding them. Embodying, as they do, an entire continuum of architectural thought, Stirling's finest works are timeless.

Jay Pritzker, J S and Philip Johnson at the award ceremony, Washington

Pritzker Prize 1981 Acceptance Speech

JAMES STIRLING

One of the continuities in the history of architecture is that every now and again a new patron and benefactor appears, and on behalf of my profession, here and abroad, I would salute Jay Pritzker - a most generous friend to architects.

Somehow I think it might have been easier for Philip Johnson who, on the first occasion of the Prize giving, talked about the importance of the new Prize to the Profession, and maybe easier for Luis Barragan - reviewing a lifetime's work. Perhaps it's more difficult for me, at any rate I feel it that way, I can't talk about the Prize as a new event and I hope I'm not at the end of my work - though I guess I'm somewhere past the midway.

It's always been difficult for me to see myself. I work very intuitively, I'm not even sure whether I'm an English architect, a European or an international architect. It is embarrassing to talk about myself and therefore I will quote from a recent article written by Robert Maxwell[1] especially about this third Pritzker award. Maxwell was a fellow student at Liverpool School of Architecture in the 1940s and is now Professor of Architecture at London University:

In England in particular there is a peculiar breath of scandal attaching to the pursuit of architecture as Art. Criticism of architecture in the public mind is broadly associated with sociological or material failure, and these spectres haunt the practice of architecture. Yet when such faults occur they are not thought to be really scandalous except when associated with high architectural aspirations.

The 'high architectural aspirations' achieved in some of our earlier projects were in a sense accidents, as the clients were not necessarily expecting a work of art in addition to a well functioning building. Buildings, which have ever since been over-run with hordes of architectural students pounding through, something the users didn't anticipate or now appreciate.

However, for me, right from the beginning the 'art' of architecture has always been **the priority**. That's what I trained to do (and incidentally it's what students are still trained to do), so it's particularly gratifying to feel that the Pritzker Prize is being awarded annually to architects who value the art as highest and who have at the same time achieved a consistent sequence of buildings.

I agree with Maxwell that by and large the UK situation is to rate artistic content as coming rather far down the line of priorities (or as something which, with a bit of luck, might just happen). So how do fine buildings get built in the UK? Often subversively, I suspect. Certainly in my earlier days it was never discussed that the buildings should also be beautiful. However, I'm pleased to say that this situation has changed and our patrons in Germany and America and our single client in the UK have commissioned us because they particularly value high quality architecture.

Historically, the quality of the art in the architecture, both at time of building and in retrospect, is remembered as the significant element. However, with the advent of modern architecture in this century, sociological, functional and real estate values have come into ascendancy. Ironically with the loss of certainty in modern architecture, the influence of Welfare State and hardnosed commercial standards is also I believe declining and the more ancient desire to see buildings wherein a primary objective is for them to appear beautiful and appropriate in their context, is returning - at least that's what my clients seem to want now.

Having stressed the importance of the art perhaps I should say where I think it's at. For many of us working with the language of abstract modern architecture, Bauhaus, international style - call it what you will - this language has become repetitive, simplistic and too narrowly confining and I for one welcome the passing of the revolutionary phase of the Modern Movement.

I think the mainstream of architecture is usually evolutionary and, though revolutions do occur along the way (and the Modern Movement was certainly one of them, as was the time of Brunelleschi), nevertheless they are minority occasions. Today we can look back and regard the whole of architectural history as our spectrum - including most certainly the Modern Movement, high tech and all. Architects have always looked back in order to move forward and we should, like painters, musicians, sculptors, etc., also be able to include representational as well as abstract elements in our art.

To quote again from Maxwell:

The risks which Stirling has been seen to take are paradoxically of two kinds, corresponding to two major phases of his career; at the beginning he was thought to be manipulating form in the name of modernity; and then, when that was finally accepted, he suddenly appeared to be manipulating it in the name of history... Modernity was never more to be a simple matter of only following function; it involved a necessary meditation on form, and on what I have called the two faces of form: the face that beckons on, and the face that looks back... There is a new kind of search for the locus of modernity in a non-utopian future.

Actually, another critic writing on our work[2] has recently perceived that there are four phases. In fact both are wrong; there is only one[3] (though our parameters are wide) and what we do now is not very different from what we have done since the beginning, though maybe there are differences in scale and materials.

So, freed from the burden of utopia but with increased responsibility, particularly in the urban and civic realm, I would like to look forward to a more liberal but equally committed professional future producing work perhaps richer in memory and association in the continuing evolution of a radical modern architecture.

Thank you.

NOTES

1 'The Pursuit of the Art of Architecture' by Robert Maxwell, May 1981, *Architectural Design* (News supplement, No. 6, 1981), reproduced here on pages 5-9.
2 'Architect for a Pluralist Age' by Martin Filler, April 1981, *Art in America*.
3 Acceptance of 1980 Royal Gold Medal in Architecture, James Stirling, *Architectural Design* 7/8 1980, reproduced here on page 12.

Cast of Henry Moore sculpture

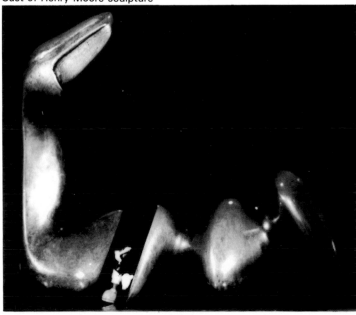

Complete List of Buildings and Projects

James Stirling

1950	Thesis
1950	Honan Competition (limited competition)
1951	Core and Crosswall House
1951	Stiff Dom-ino Housing
1951	ICA Furniture
1952	Poole Technical College (national competition)
1953	Sheffield University (national competition with Alan Cordingley)
1953	House in North London
1954	Woolton House
1955	Village Project (Team X)

James Stirling and James Gowan

1955-58	Ham Common Flats
1956-58	Isle of Wight House
1956	House Studies
1956	House in the Chilterns
1957	Three houses for B. Mavrolean family (limited competition)
1957-59	House Conversion, Kensington
1957	Expandable House
1957-59	Preston Infill Housing (tender cost competition)
1958	Steel Mill Cladding
1958	Churchill College (limited competition)
1958-61	School Assembly Hall, Camberwell
1959	Selwyn College
1959-63	Leicester University Engineering Building
1960-64	Old Peoples Home
1960-64	Childrens Home

James Stirling

1964-67	Cambridge University History Building (limited competition)
1964-68	Flats at Camden Town
1964-68	Residential Expansion: St. Andrews University
1965	Dorman Long HQ
1966-71	Queen's College Oxford

1967-76	Runcorn New Town Housing
1968	Redevelopment Study, New York USA (with A. Baker)
1969-76	Low Cost Housing, Lima, Peru (limited competition)
1969-72	Olivetti Training School, Haslemere
1969	Siemens AG Munich (limited competition)
1970	Derby Town Centre (limited competition)

James Stirling and Michael Wilford

1971	Olivetti HQ, Milton Keynes
1971	Arts Centre, St. Andrews University
1972-77	Southgate Housing, Rucorn
1975	Museum for Northrhine Westphalia, Düsseldorf (invited competition)
1975	Wallraf-Richartz Museum, Cologne (invited competition)
1976	Meineke Strasse, Berlin
1976	Government Centre. Doha (limited competition)
1976	Regional Centre for Tuscany (national competition with Castore, Malanima, Rizzi)
1977	Revisions to the Nolli Plan for Rome
1977	Dresdner Bank, Marburg, Germany
1977	Housing Study of Muller Pier, Rotterdam
1977-83	Staatsgalerie New Building and Chamber Theatre, Stuttgart (limited competition)
1978	Institute of Biology and Biochemistry, Tehran, Iran (in association with Burckhardt and Partner)
1978	Bayer AG, PF Zentrum, Monheim, Germany (limited competition)
1978	15 Luxury Houses, Manhattan, New York
1979-81	Rice University, Houston, USA: extension of School of Architecture
1979-84	Wissenschaftszentrum Berlin (limited competition)
1979-84	Fogg Museum New Building, Harvard University, USA
1980	Columbia University, New York, Chemistry Dept.
1980-84	Turner Museum and Tate Gallery Expansion, London
1980	Extensions to the Music School and Plaza, and Ministry Offices and Gallery, Stuttgart
1981	Houston Plaza, USA

Biographical Notes

| 1926 | Born Glasgow (family moved to Liverpool 1927) |

EDUCATION
1942	Liverpool School of Art
1945-50	Liverpool University, School of Architecture: Dipl Arch (dist)
1949	Student exchange to New York, USA
1950-52	School of Town Planning & Regional Research, London

DESIGN AND PROFESSIONAL EXPERIENCE
| 1953-56 | Senior Assistant with Lyons, Israel and Ellis |
| 1956 | Private Practice (Partner: James Gowan until 1963; Michael Wilford from 1971) |

GENERAL
1969	Honorary Member of the Akademie der Kunste, Berlin
1973	BBC/Arts Council Film - 'James Stirling's Architecture'
1975	IUA Congress Madrid and Barcelona
1976	Honorary Fellow, American Institute of Architects
1976	Brunner Award, the National Institute of Arts and Letters, USA
1977	Alvar Aalto Award, Helsinki
1979	Honorary Member of the Florence Academy of Arts
1979	Honorary Doctorate, Royal College of Art
1979	Fellow of the Royal Society of Arts, London
1979	Honorary Member of the Academia Nazionale San Luca, Italy
1980	Royal Gold Medal for Architecture, RIBA
1981	The Pritzker Prize, USA

EXHIBITIONS
1969	*James Stirling — Three Buildings* Museum of Modern Art, New York
1974	Drawings Exhibition, RIBA Heinz Gallery, London
1975	*19 Projects* — Travelling Exhibition (initiated by Naples University and British Council). Exhibited in Naples, Rome, Brussels, Zurich, Lausanne, Trieste, Tehran
1976	*9 Architects* Dortmund University
1976	Venice Biennale
1977	Via Arte Della Lana, Sanmichele, Florence (Florence project)
1977	*Architecture 1* Leo Castelli Gallery, New York 1977 (architectural drawings)
1978	Roma Interrotta, Rome (Nolli plans)
1979	*Museum Projects* Dortmund University
1980	*Manhattan Townhouses*, Richard Meier/James Stirling, The Lobby Gallery, New York
1980	*Three German Projects* RIBA, London
1981	Drawings of the new extension, Fogg Museum, Cambridge, Mass, USA

SELECTED WORK
1950-1980

Side stepping staircase,
Queen's College, Oxford, 1966

1951
Core and Crosswall House
James Stirling

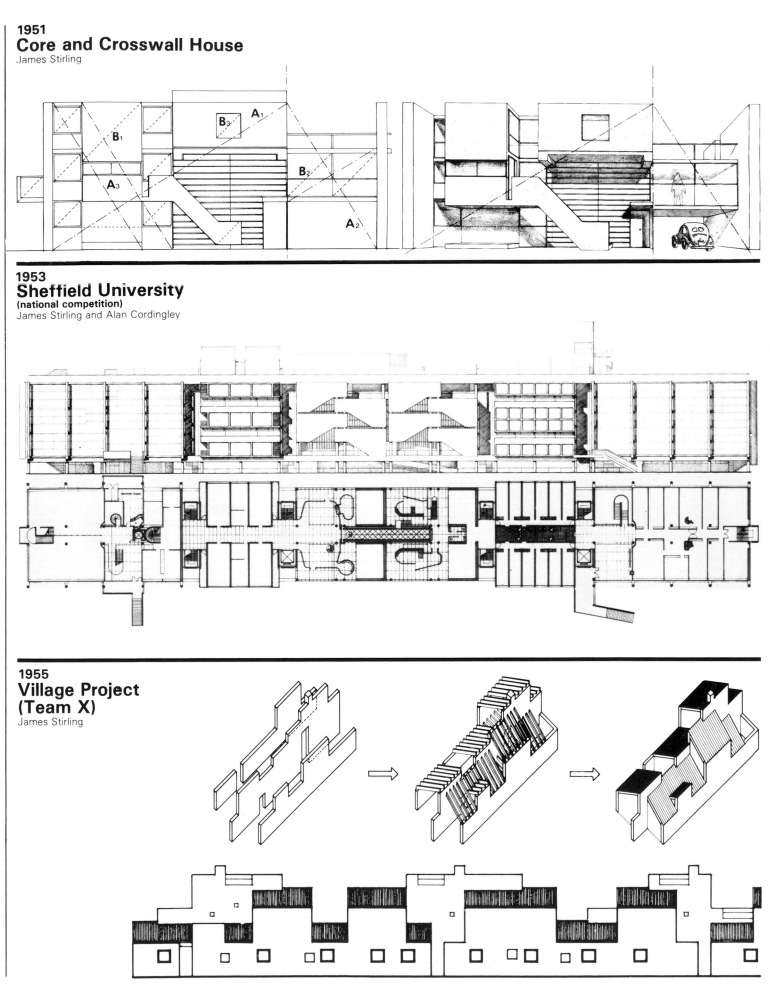

1953
Sheffield University
(national competition)
James Stirling and Alan Cordingley

1955
Village Project
(Team X)
James Stirling

1955-58
Ham Common Flats
James Stirling and James Gowan
David Walsby

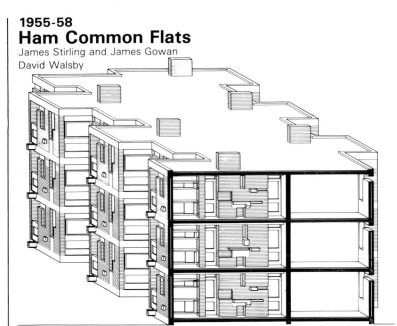

1956

House in the Chilterns
James Stirling and James Gowan

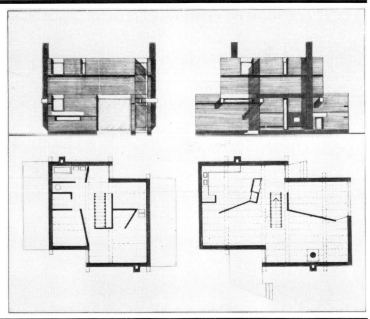

1957
Three Houses for B. Mavrolean family
(limited competition)
James Stirling
and James Gowan

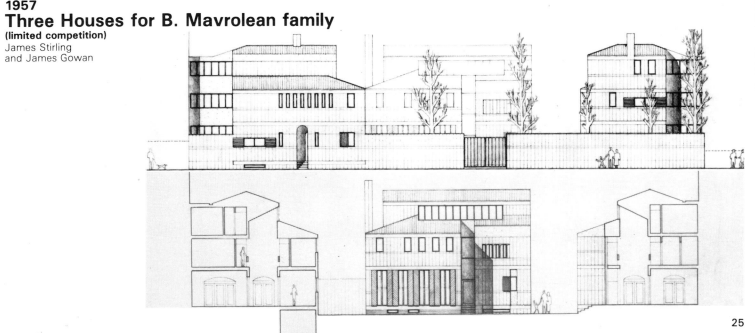

1957-59
Preston Infill Housing
(tender cost competition)
James Stirling and James Gowan
David Walsby
John Turner & Sons

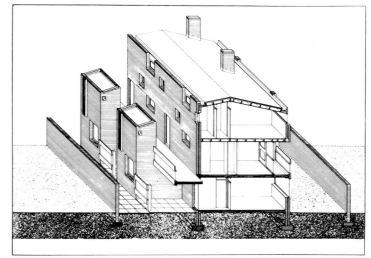

1958
Churchill College
(limited competition)
James Stirling and James Gowan
Kit Evans, Malcolm Higgs, David Gray

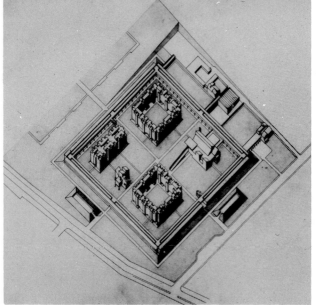

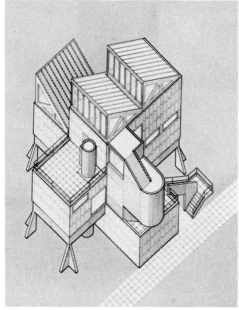

1958-61
School Assembly Hall, Camberwell

James Stirling and James Gowan
Kenneth Davis
F.J. Samuely & Partners

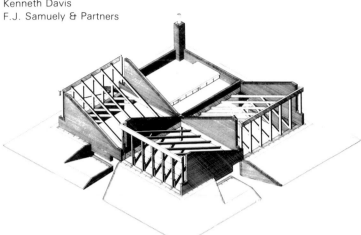

1959
Selwyn College

James Stirling and James Gowan

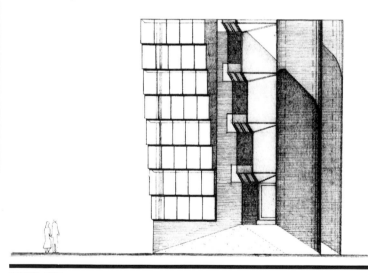

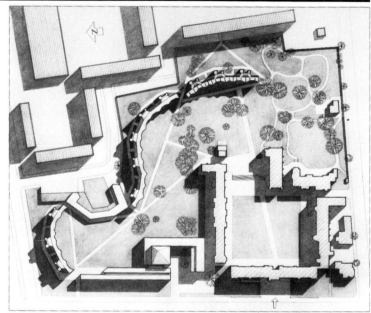

1959-63
Leicester University Engineering Building

James Stirling and James Gowan
Michael Wilford, Malcolm Higgs
F.J. Samuely & Partners
Steensen, Varming & Mulcahy
Monk & Dunstone

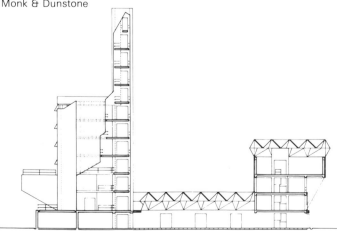

Research Laboratories,
Leicester University Engineering
Building, 1959-63

1960-64
Childrens Home
James Stirling and James Gowan
Roy Cameron

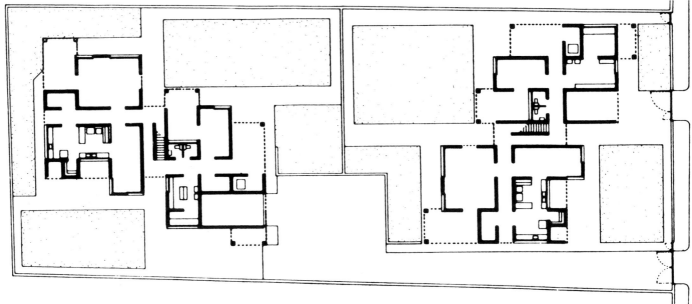

1964-67
Cambridge University
History Building
(limited competition)
James Stirling
Michael Wilford, Brian Frost,
David Bartlett
F.J. Samuely & Partners
R.W. Gregory & Partners
Monk & Dunstone

Reading Library,
Cambridge University History
Building, 1964-67

1964-68
Residential Expansion:
St Andrews University

James Stirling

Brian Frost, David Bartlett, Alfred Bews

F.J. Samuely & Partners
Ewbank & Partners
Monk & Dunstone

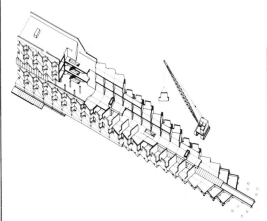

1966-71
Queen's College Oxford

James Stirling

Roy Cameron, Gunther Ismer

F.J. Samuely & Partners
Bressloff Associates
Monk & Dunstone

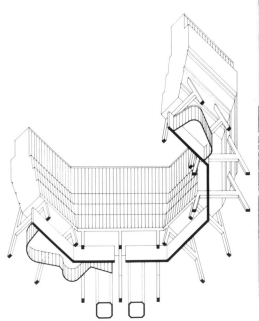

1967-76
Runcorn New Town Housing

James Stirling

Michael Wilford, Julian Harrap, David Gibson,
David Bartlett, Peter Ray, Robin Nicholson,
David Falck, Tony Smith, David St. John

F.J. Samuely & Partners
Davis, Belfield & Everest

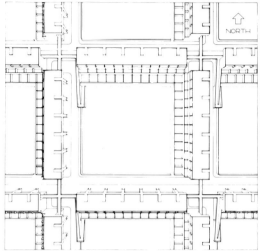

1969-72
Olivetti Training School, Haslemere

James Stirling

Robin Nicholson, David Weinberg,
David Falck, Barbara Littenberg

F.J. Samuely & Partners
Dale & Ewbank
Monk & Dunstone
Polyplan Ltd.

1969
Siemens AG Munich
(limited competition)
James Stirling
Leon Krier, Michael Lehmbrock,
Oswald Zoeggeler

1970
Derby Town Centre
(limited competition)

James Stirling

Leon Krier

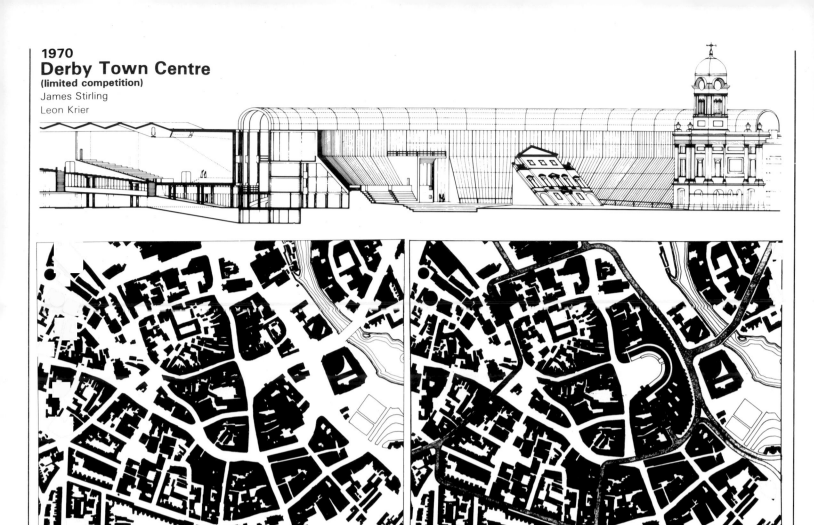

1971
Arts Centre
St Andrews University

James Stirling and Michael Wilford

Crispin Osborne, Julian Harrap,
Werner Kreis

F.J. Samuely & Partners

Dale & Ewbank

Monk & Dunstone

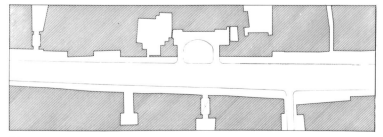

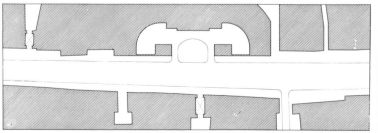

1975

Museum for Northrhine Westphalia, Düsseldorf
(invited competition)

James Stirling and Michael Wilford

Russell Bevington, Robert Livesey,
Crispin Osborne

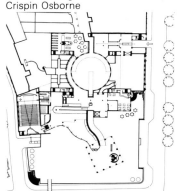

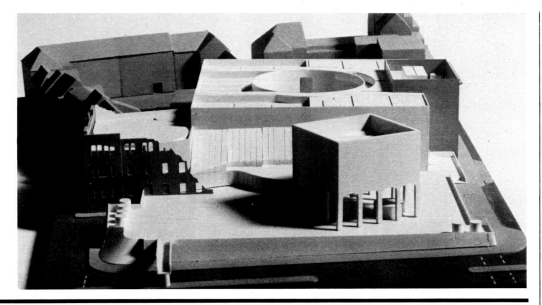

1975

Wallraf-Richartz Museum, Cologne
(invited competition)

James Stirling and Michael Wilford

Russell Bevington, Robert Livesey,
Werner Kreis, Ulrich Schaad

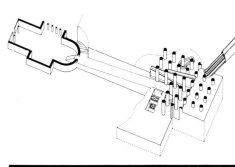

1976

Meineke Strasse, Berlin

James Stirling and Michael Wilford
Ulrich Schaad

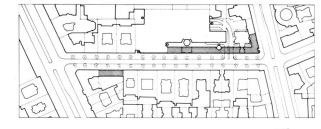

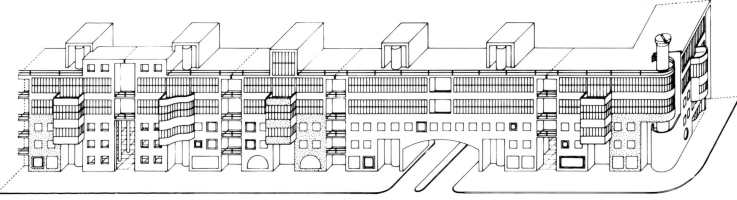

1976
Government Centre, Doha
(limited competition)

James Stirling and Michael Wilford

Russell Bevington, John Tuomey

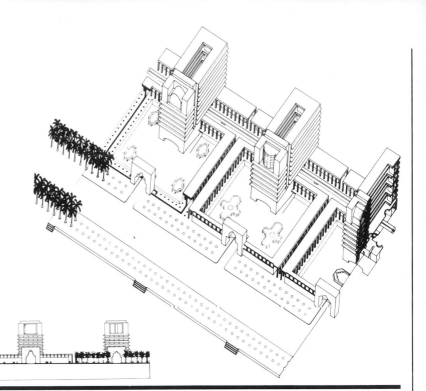

1976
Regional Centre for Tuscany
(national competition)

James Stirling and Michael Wilford in collaboration with Castore, Malanima and Rizzi.

Russell Bevington, Ulrich Schaad, John Tuomey, Barbara Weiss

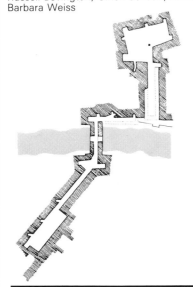

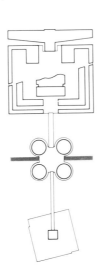

1977
Dresdner Bank, Marburg, Germany

James Stirling and Michael Wilford

Ulrich Schaad

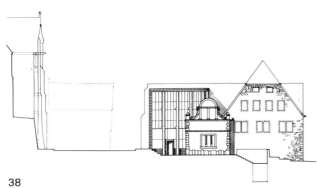

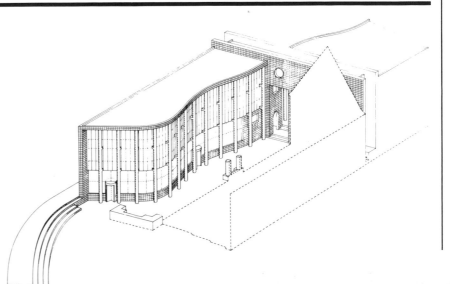

1977
DRESDNER BANK
Marburg Germany

James Stirling and Michael Wilford
Ulrich Schaad

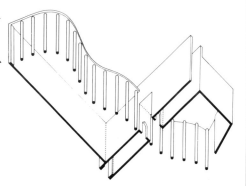

The new building replaces the existing much modified and ruined building that flanks Pilgrimstein and will contain a bank at ground level with offices above. At second floor level there could be self-contained professional offices. The new building will be orientated towards the medieval mill and away from the heavily trafficked street (noise etc.) and the interspace between the new building and the old mill is designed as a meandering pedestrian passageway similar to the many footways in Marburg, in particular to the nearby footpath descending into Pilgrimstein from the old town centre. The new passageway is also an arcade or semi-covered way appropriate to commercial requirements.

The pavement which is to be added by the City to the north side of the Weidenhauser bridge will connect with the existing pavement around the old mill and from this there would be steps down to a slightly lower general level. This lower level better relates the Renaissance gable to a ground surface (at the moment it has a sinking feeling) and at the same time reduces the number of steps up from the pedestrian underpass.

At the opposite end of the old mill the existing extension would be replaced by a new building (shop) which continues the passageway/arcade concept and the curving arcade outside this shop could be used for window shopping and as a shelter for people waiting for buses - which may become more necessary if this area is developed for bus parking.

The arched niches in the facade of Pilgrimstein are a 'memory' of the arches under the clock tower which was a feature of the rebuilding at the turn of the century (when half of the original mill was taken down). These arches were greatly reduced when the tower was recently cut in half to make way for post-war road widening.

The exterior of the old mill (16th century) should be converted to its original form as far as is practical.

By the design of the new building and passageway both the old mill and the Renaissance gable are better displayed to the public.

An everyday use should be found for the old mill — for instance as museum/gallery or restaurant, alternatively as office/public user space, i.e: Telephone Authority. It might also be used as classroom/studio space for education/art purposes or possibly converted for dance or small scale theatre. Conversion proposals for the old mill are not shown pending a decision on its intended use (on going to press the mill was to be converted for use as a repertory theatre). However, a new entrance into the old mill could be made from the passageway and this is shown on the drawings.

The design of the new building utilises the architectural and urban language of Marburg. Elements include: meandering footway, arcade, brick and tiled walls, structural facade, buttress (the service wall). This last element maintains a reason for the bending of the road in Pilgrimstein which at the moment attractively partially encloses the south view towards Rudolphsplatz (this partial closure occurs with the existing building and in our opinion should be continued with the new building).

James Stirling, 1977

Notes
1 Within the 'service wall' it is possible to plan various combinations of entrance separations. The employees entrance to the bank could be made self contained.
2 The large display cabinet backed onto the north side of the 'service wall' is for displaying goods from the shop.
3 The colonnade adjoining the shop defines the start of the pedestrian passageway and also acts as a barrier or screen to the adjoining pavement area which could be used for car-parking.
4 The external finish shown on the drawings is of tiles with a surface texture similar to that of brickwork.

Expansion of the roadworks and degeneration of the Alt Mill in the 16th, 17th and 20th centuries

Site axonometric

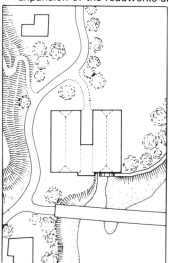
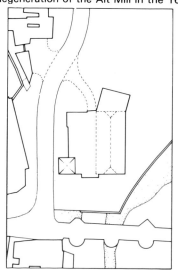
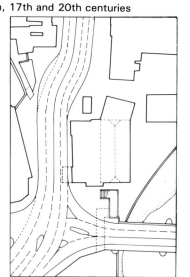
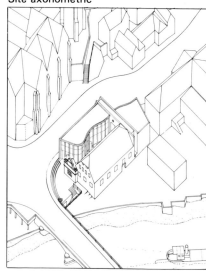

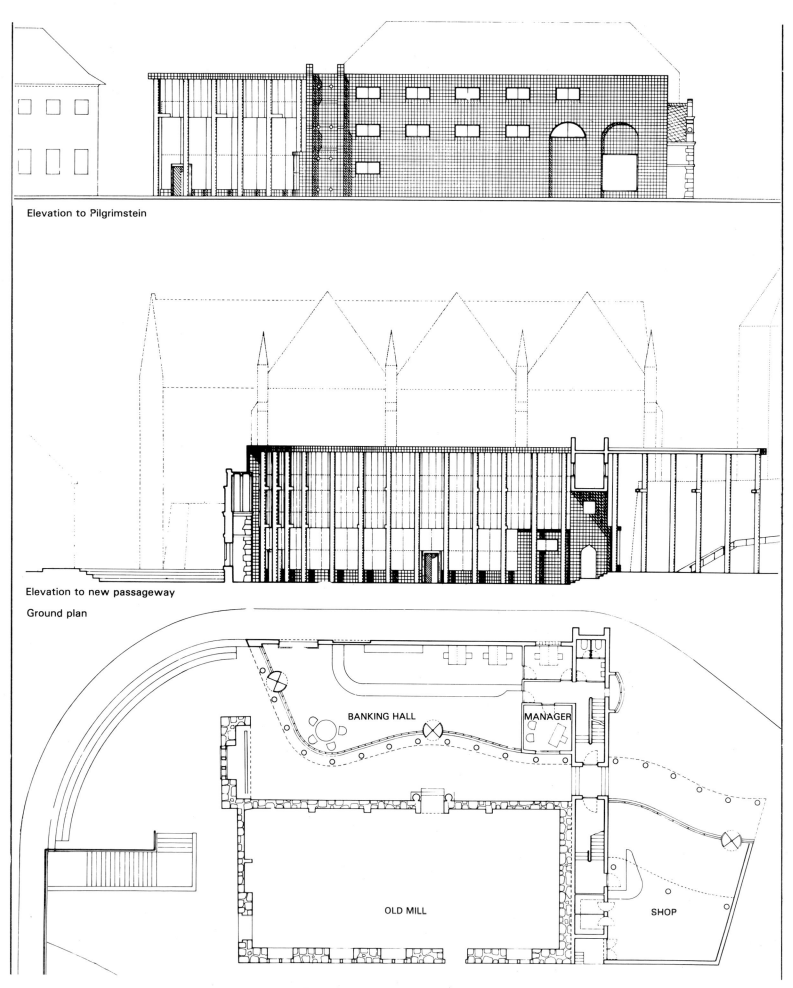

Elevation to Pilgrimstein

Elevation to new passageway

Ground plan

BANKING HALL

MANAGER

OLD MILL

SHOP

41

1978
BAYER AG P F ZENTRUM
Monheim Germany

James Stirling and Michael Wilford

Alexis Pontvik, Alan Levitt

SITE LAYOUT

Buildings are sited with the intention of creating an idyllic Research and Development Centre and it is hoped to achieve an arcadian setting for the whole complex with perhaps similar building-to-landscape relationships as were achieved in the 18th century with the large country house (or Schloss) and its attendant outbuildings set amid picturesque landscape.

The Laboratory Complexes are positioned radially around a landscaped park and each is planned as a group of buildings around internal gardens. The entrance facades which overlook the park would be completed in the first construction phase and the 150% future expansion requirement is provided by extending the complex in an outward direction — increasing by whatever amount in any time phasing. The identity of the Centre buildings and the integration of the Laboratory Complexes would be established at the outset and be preserved through all stages of subsequent development. Overall we hope to avoid the institutional and we are attempting to achieve a visual integration of sophisticated/technical with vernacular/rusticated. Staff and visitors using the lounges, arcaded corridors and internal gardens should feel that what they are experiencing is more akin to a sequence of Florentine courtyards and gardens than the entirely functional environment of an anonymous Research Centre.

The Administration offices are at the mid point adjoining the site entrance and are contained in a U-shaped building which is positioned as a focal point, spatially counter-balancing the radiating Laboratory Complexes. A Conference Centre is located in the base of this U-shaped Office Building and other Central Facilities are planned in wings extending either side.

Access is past the entrance lodges into an Entrance Plaza from which there is direct entry into the Administration building, also down stepped ramps into the park. Prior to reaching the Entrance Plaza, all service traffic, including staff cars are deflected to flanking service roads.

The Park is a garden of relaxation and spaciousness for the everyday use of staff and would be walked through en-route to the Dining rooms, Library, Conference Area and offices etc. The ground is formed as a shallow bowl with many groupings of specimen and exotic trees and the edge of the Park is defined by a canal with parallel lines of trees. Footbridges over this canal lead into garden pavilions (gazebos) which mark the entrance of each Laboratory Complex. The Park could be open to the public on an occasional or continuous basis and would require minimal

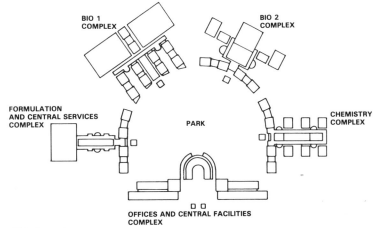

Site layout

supervision if gates were installed on the footbridges to prevent the public from wandering into the Laboratory Complexes.

Traffic enters (and exits) the site through a single control point — at the entrance lodges — and immediately connects with the roads that link the Entrance Plaza, the perimeter service roads and the tree-lined avenue around the Park. Access to staff car parking service areas and test fields is via the perimeter service road. Layby car parking for visitors to the Laboratory Complexes is provided on the tree lined avenue adjacent to the entrance pavilions. Laboratory staff parking is in three large tree-shaded car parks positioned between Complexes. Conference, office staff and visitors' parking is housed in two multi-level car parks positioned either side of the Entrance Plaza.

ADMINISTRATION OFFICES AND CENTRAL FACILITIES

The Conference reception and lounges can be approached from the Entrance Plaza by crossing the courtyard formed by the U-shaped Administration Building. Elevator lobbies serving the office floors also overlook the Entrance Plaza.

In wings either side of the Administration Building are located the Library, Exhibition Hall, Tropicarium, Cafeteria and Dining Rooms — all overlooking the Park. These facilities are inter-connected by rooflit gallerias which contain staircases that provide access to the multi-level car parks.

Site plan

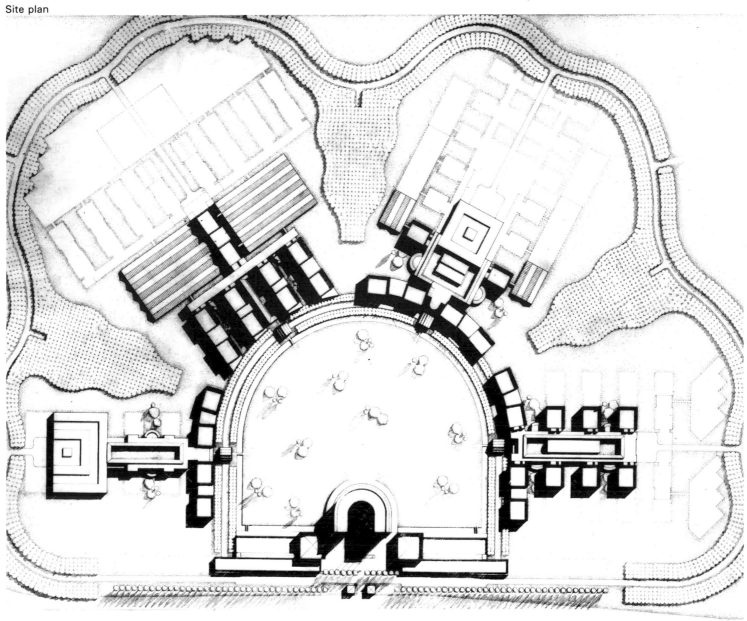

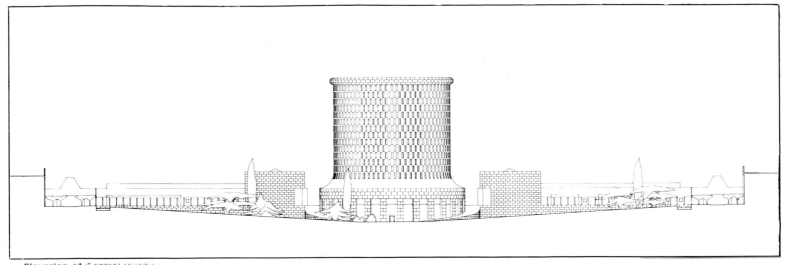

Elevation of Central Building

Section/elevation of Central Building

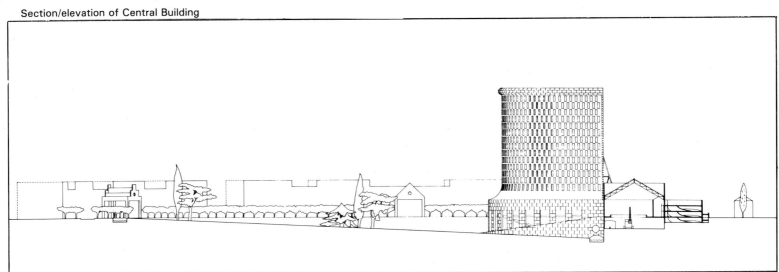

Plan of Central Building

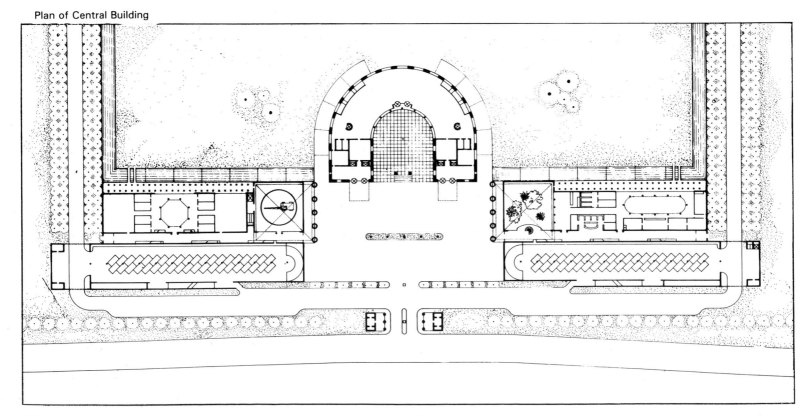

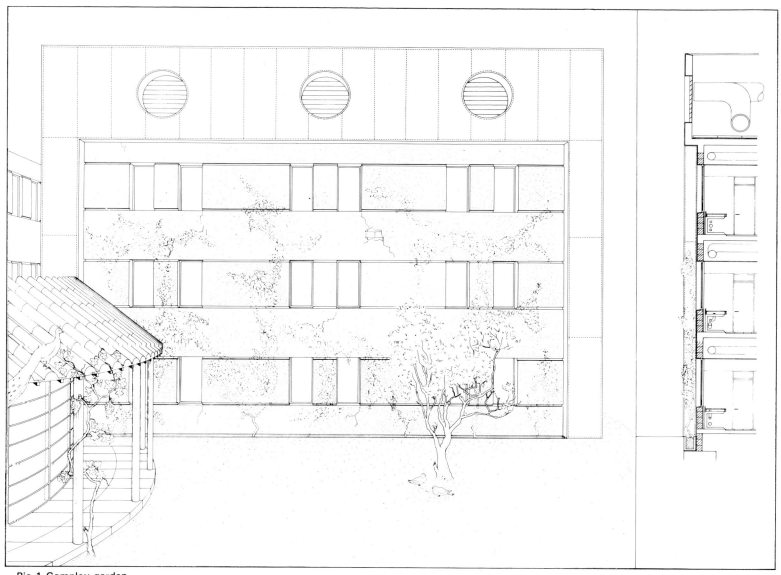

Bio 1 Complex garden

Bio 1 Complex

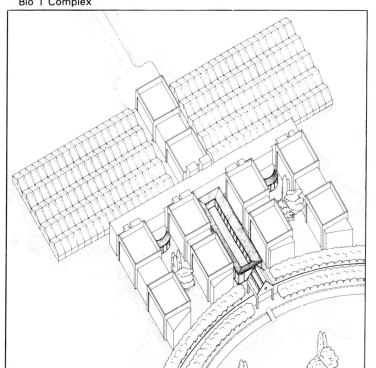

Bio 2 Complex

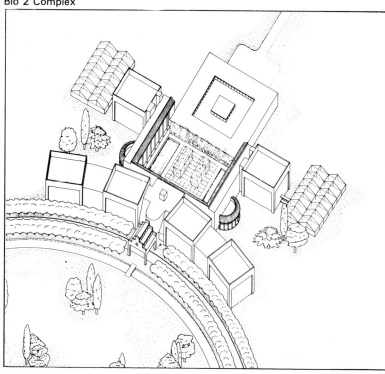

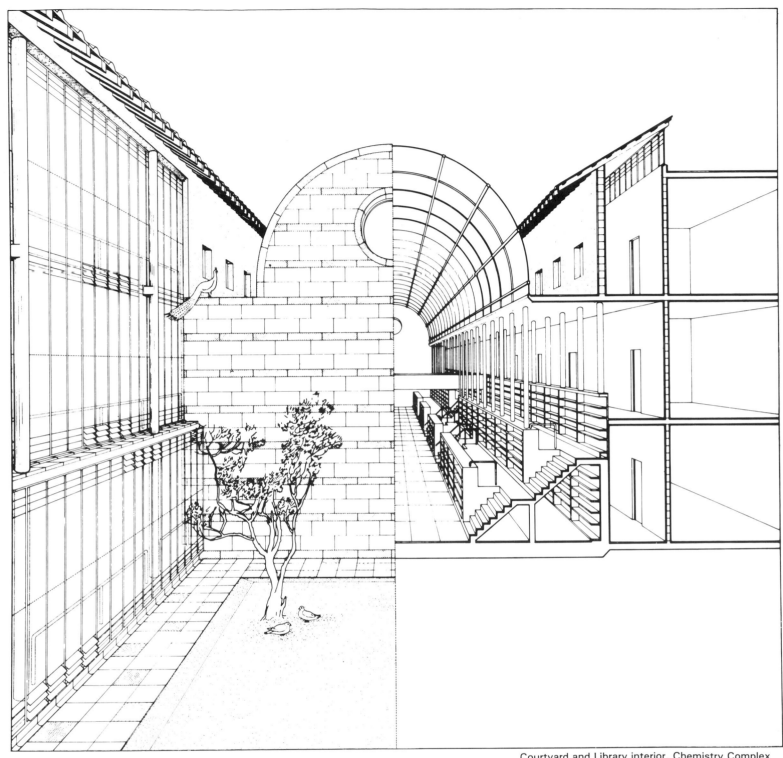

Courtyard and Library interior, Chemistry Complex

LABORATORY COMPLEXES
Primary circulation routes extend from the garden entrance pavilion like spines, down the length of each Complex, with short subsidiary corridors serving the laboratory blocks. Staff entrances at the ends of the laboratory blocks permit short walking distances to staff car parks. Service docks are located at the ends of the spinal circulation.

The blocks of heavily serviced laboratories are planned on three levels with adjoining ancillary areas. General offices and unspecialised accommodation is usually located off the spinal circulation including at ground level the staff lounges with verandas and terraces overlooking gardens.

CHEMISTRY
The Library which is at the core of this Complex can be entered along both flanks allowing convenient access from all departments. The Reading Room is daylit through a vaulted glass roof and bookstacks are arranged in three tiers on each side with archive storage below. Flanking arcades continue beyond the ends of the Library to form courtyard gardens and interconnect with the laboratory blocks.

BIOLOGY 1
The entry lobby is linked to the entrance pavilion by a short colonnade. Control departments are positioned on the spinal circulation and there are connections to the greenhouses.

BIOLOGY 2
A central courtyard containing a nuclear pool and an island terrace for birdcages is enclosed by three levels of arcades. This courtyard

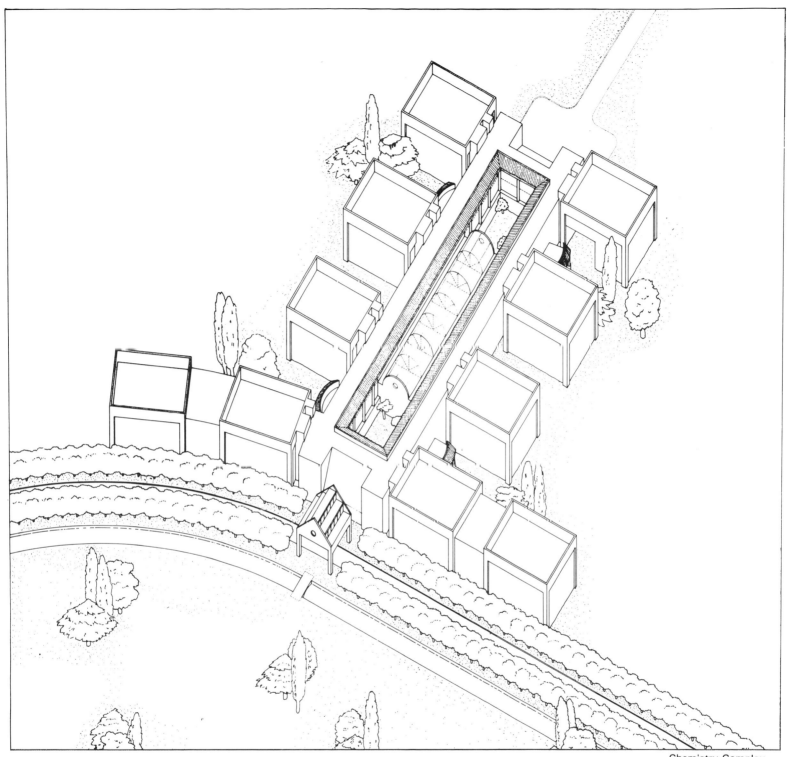

Chemistry Complex

island provides a secure area for outside experiments and tests involving nuclear materials.

MATERIALS AND CONSTRUCTION
Laboratory Blocks
The external surface is of plaster/rendering arranged in horizontal bands down the facade in two colours. Colour combinations change with each Complex. The corner *legs* and the walls above roof level enclosing the service area are of pressed metal sheeting with blue enamel or anodised finish. In contrast to the high tech finish of these laboratory blocks the social areas, corridors and general rooms are of vernacular appearance with sloping roofs carried on timber joists surfaced in traditional Roman or ceramic rooftiles. Stone facing is used on special areas, such as the end walls of the Library.

Central Administration
These buildings are of reinforced concrete beam and column construction with block infill walls. The external surface is a combination of mustard coloured rendering and a veneer of light grey sandstone.

SERVICES
Separate ventilation equipment etc. for each Laboratory block is on the roof and this open service area is enclosed by full height walls allowing maximum change and flexibility in the adjustment of rooftop equipment without this frequent process being visible. The *legs* at the corners of each laboratory block are fresh air supply ducts.

JS/MW & A

1977-83
STAATSGALERIE NEW BUILDING AND CHAMBER THEATRE
Stuttgart Germany

James Stirling and Michael Wilford
LONDON OFFICE
Ulrich Schaad, Russell Bevington, Peter Ray, Alexis Pontvik, John Tuomey,
John Cannon, Markus Geiger, Paul Keogh, John Cairns, Ulrike Wilke,
Alfred Munkenbeck, Peter Schaad, Shinichi Tomoe, Chris MacDonald
STUTTGART OFFICE
Siggi Wernik, Tommi Tafel, Rudolf Schwarz, Pia Riegert, Laszlo Glaser,
Jochen Bub, Heribert Hamann, Christian Ohm

In 1974 a national competition was initiated by Baden-Württemberg for building designs and urban proposals along the zone of Konrad Adenauerstrasse south of the existing Staatsgalerie in Stuttgart. This included designs for the Gallery extension and nine architects were awarded places. In 1977 another competition was held specifically for the design of the Staatsgalerie extension and the Chamber Theatre. In addition to the previous nine German firms, four foreign architects were invited to take part. The jury numbered 18 and included the directors of the Gallery and Theatre, the rector of the Music School, the Minister of Finance, the Bürgermeister, town planning officials, etc., and six architect jurors.

Extracts from Competition Report:
SITE LAYOUT AND TOWN PLANNING
Objectives:
1 To bring the public moving diagonally across the site into meaningful contact with the new building - neither sub-dividing the site with the required new public footpath nor committing people to pass along the back of a building. This 'urban type' route therefore passes at high level (outside of security) around the Sculpture Yard and down to the entrance terrace then through the Theatre arch to the corner of Eugenstrasse. It is hoped that this routing will stimulate people to visit the Gallery.
2 To continue a 3m high landscaped terrace (town planning suggestion) along Konrad Adenauerstrasse and allow the possibility for a footbridge across Eugenstrasse thus providing uninterrupted pedestrian flow. Directly off this terrace (car park under) are the public entrances to the Gallery and Theatre. This arrangement respects the historic relationship of public buildings facing a Mall (Konrad Adenauerstrasse).
3 By design of the new building, respect the frontalising characteristic of the Staatsgalerie and Staatstheater and by siting of the Theatre wing allow the possibility for a new urban square on Eugenstrasse. This square faces the portal of the Staatstheater and its south side could be formed by the proposed office building. The frontalising aspect suggests across axes over Konrad Adenauerstrasse and (if this road goes underground) could be a basis for the design of landscape and planting. This axiality supports the intention of developing stronger linkages between the Palace gardens and the hillside.
4 To reinforce the traditional relationship of buildings to street by retaining all existing buildings on Urbanstrasse and Eugenstrasse so maintaining the street character of this area.

5 By alignment and height of the Administration/Library block, better establish the square on Urbanplatz which could be further improved by extending the diagonal route of existing roads and by pushing into the square the informal landscape which is descending the hill.

NEW GALLERY EXTENSION
Objectives:
1 To create a sequence of well-defined and well-proportioned Gallery 'rooms', avoiding 'endless flexible space' or gymnastic roof sections. The ceilings of these rooms would be a flat surface of diffusing glass, allowing passage of shadowless natural light - similar to the existing Staatsgaleries but more rationalised. The Gallery rooms have several possibilities for varied layout of partition walls.
2 To achieve a chronological 'journey' through the history of painting and sculpture, either with a journey from 'present to past' beginning in the new building, or a journey from 'past to present' beginning in the old building.
3 To allow the public to flow without physical or psychological break between the new building and the old building - hence no change in floor level or awareness of crossing a bridge.
4 The Sculpture Yard ('encircled inner court') is also the way up to additional sculpture terraces at Gallery floor level - the exhibiting of sculpture was regarded as 'a special design feature'. As these terraces are within security, the public could in good weather pass through glazed doors (occurring in several Gallery rooms) allowing an informal strolling in-and-out use. A centrally positioned revolving door would allow the public to inspect sculpture in all weather conditions.
5 The cafeteria is related to and links entrance areas of both the Gallery and Theatre and special lock doors could control single or dual entry. The cafeteria is slightly oversize allowing a spatial passage between Theatre and Gallery. It seemed more relevant to relate the cafeteria to the public/entrance terrace than to an internal sculpture yard in particular to support and activate events on the terrace, such as happenings, temporary exhibitions etc. Service to cafe tables on the terrace would be possible.
6 The administration is located in the upper levels of the building facing Urbanstrasse from which there is a separate non-public staff entrance. At the lower levels of this block is the library which is accessible to the public from the gallery entrance hall via a ramped corridor that overlooks the sculpture yard.

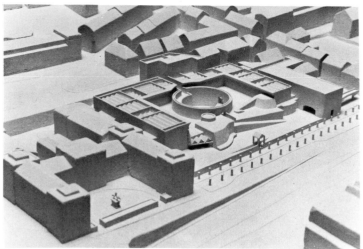

'frontalising axiality'

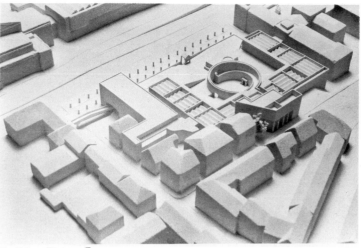

'building to street'

CHAMBER THEATRE
Objectives:
1 To site the new Chamber Theatre close to the Staatstheater.
2 To achieve the 'dream configuration' (suggested in the programme requirements) of all theatre spaces being in line without detrimental effect to town planning considerations and green zone requirements. The end of this block incorporates a wide arch over the pedestrian route. This arch would identify the Theatre, in place of the traditional entrance canopy or portico and provide an element of sequence in the linear walkway along the green zone. The arch also acts to introduce the new Gallery, similar to the passage opening under the south wing of the existing Gallery. A public box (ticket) office is located under the Theatre arch; it could function when the theatre is not in use.

MUSIC SCHOOL
Objectives:
1 To be located near the Music Academy in Urbanplatz and have a separate entrance. Also to be sited away from traffic noise and planned to avoid acoustic disturbance to the Gallery or Theatre.
2 For the accommodation to be eventually accessible to the Gallery (by opening of built-in pass doors) and similarly for it to retain later use possibilities for the Theatre.

STRUCTURE, SERVICES AND MATERIALS
The structure for the whole complex would be of reinforced concrete with structural walls and columns. At first floor a deep coffered slab allows for the spanning of large ground floor areas such as the Lecture Theatre and Exhibition Gallery without intermediary columns. The roofs over the Gallery rooms and the Theatre are spanned with steel trusses.

The horizontal run of services (including air conditioning) is accommodated within the deep coffered slab and the roof space afforded by the trusses. The cornice which runs around the courtyard side of the galleries also acts as a horizontal duct.

External walls would be veneered with natural or reconstructed stone, with similar paving to terraces. In general, internal walls would be white painted on plaster. The exterior finish of the Administration Block would be of rendering. With further development an intention would be to confine the stonework to the Gallery only, with the adjoining pavilions of the Chamber Theatre, Music School and Administration Block having a rendered external finish.

JS/MW & A

Site plan

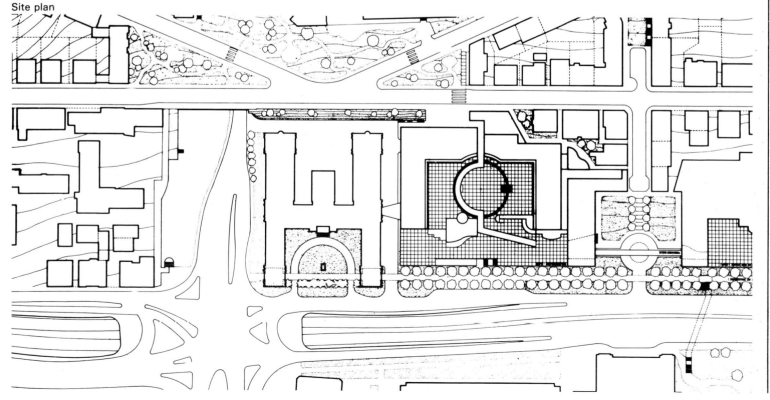

JS
78

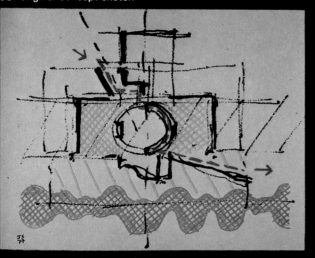

A NOTE ON THE DRAWINGS

CHARLES JENCKS

These coloured drawings clarify the design intentions behind the museum and theatre. Above all they accentuate the dualisms inherent in the design, the juxtaposition of rectangle and circle, frontality and rotation, axiality and diagonality, and also the attitude of collage, the idea that the new buildings should both support and contrast with the existing urban fabric.

Dualism, with its intrinsic binary logic, is quite obviously a rhetorical device (and necessity) of communication. The rectangular layout of the picture gallery is broken by the circular sculptural court, just as the latter is broken by rectangular holes of circulation, and in both cases these emphasised juxtapositions increase our perception of the forms *per se*. In like manner the juxtaposation of primary colour canopies against a more neutral masonry background heightens the identity of each element. They are, as it were, de Stijl canopies of steel and glass collaged onto a Schinkelesque background (which conforms with the local Stuttgart fabric). This is not then a Neoclassical approach

50

Up view of gallery entrance and
canopy. Entrance is off a
terrace fronting on to Konrad
Adenauerstrasse. The carpark is
underneath.

JS
78

Full frontal up view of gallery
entrance. Stone veneer on
concrete walls. The stonework
is alternating bands of
travertine and sandstone, both
local to Stuttgart.

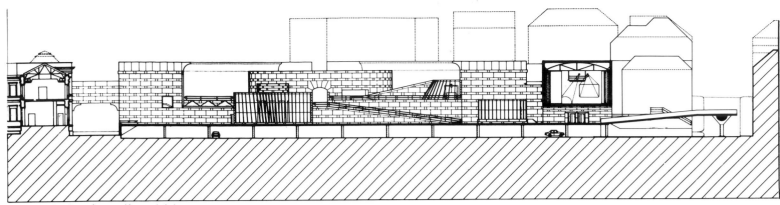

Elevation/section to Konrad Adenauerstrasse

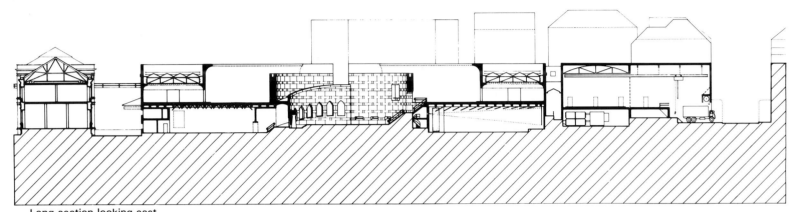

Long section looking east

Entrance level plan

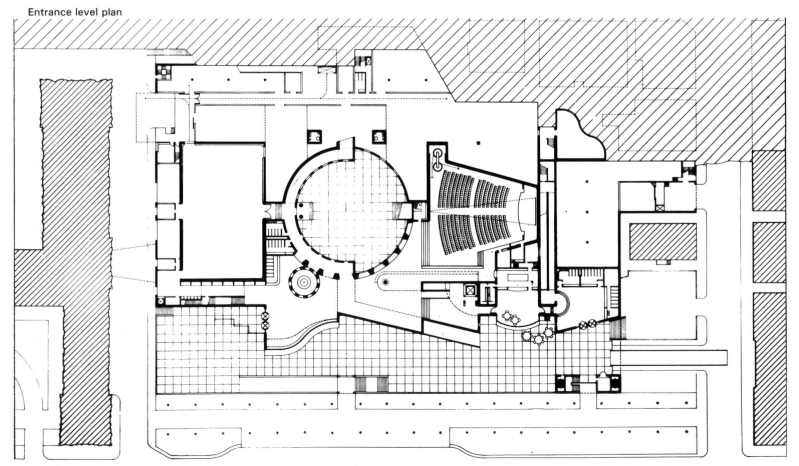

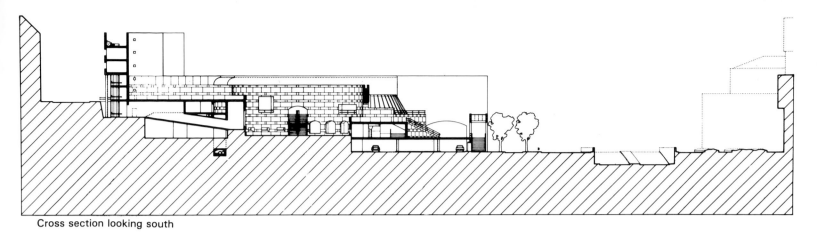

Cross section looking south

Cross section looking north

Gallery level plan

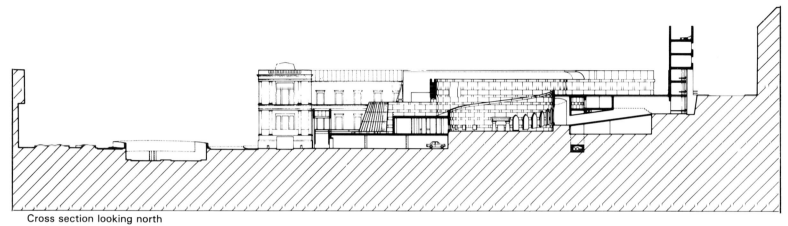

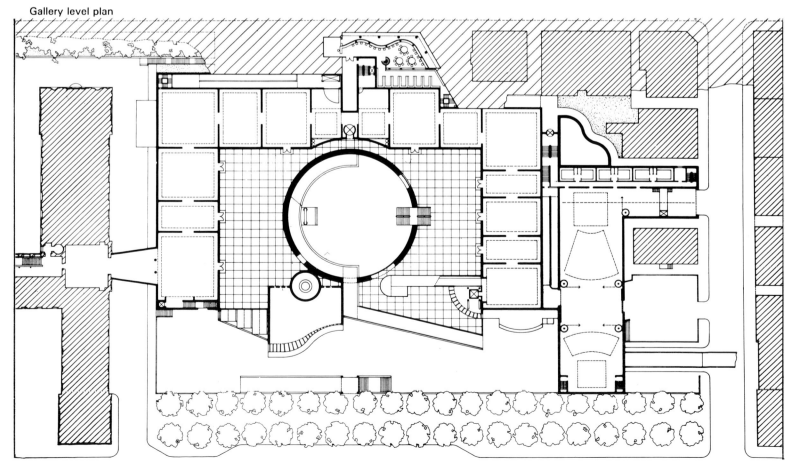

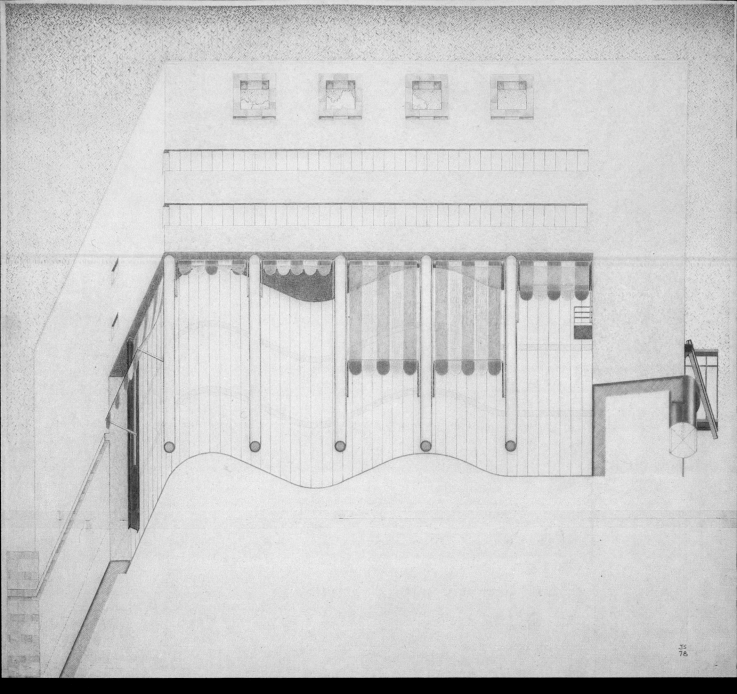

although some elements of this style are used. A Neo-Classicist would play down the oppositions and integrate the canopies in form, colour and material. A collagist, by contrast, takes forms and ideas from heterogeneous sources, preserves a minimal identity and semantic meaning, and then by juxtaposition creates a new set of meanings at odds with the original ones.

It is this particular aspect of the duality which is most apparent in the drawings. Some people might find them perverse or at least incongruous. What is the Machine Aesthetic doing on a Schinkelesque facade, with such obvious discontinuity? Whereas Mies or Philip Johnson might mix the two aesthetics and two semantics, they would not violently contrast them in colour and texture. Perhaps there is here an allusion to the two German realities (not East and West), the cultural and technological, both of which explicitly use these two semantic systems as a matter of course; and perhaps the building can be seen as a systematic confrontation of these two cultures with neither of them gaining an easy and predictable victory. With this supposition in mind we might compare these drawings to the *ad hoc* amalgams of Viollet-le-Duc. The latter were also 'rational' confrontations of two

separate realms claiming authority, the traditional and the techno logical, and they were also experienced as incongruous - ever today by critics such as John Summerson.

The ornamental treatment, such as it is, also breaks customary rules of composition, while retaining some. Flat arches are punched through levels of banded masonry, without transition or mouldings. Whereas some walls, windows, cornices and rustication follow the usual classical conventions, others do not We have, once again, some Neoclassical elements abruptly torn cut out, or superimposed according to collagist principles. Thus the scheme is actually more provocative than the straightforward contextualist project that it first appears to be. It does fit into the fabric and knit it together, but with a richer language than the Neo classical. It speaks, as dual structures do, on two quite distinct levels, offering a reconciliation with tradition and context on the one hand, and a confrontration of cultures on the other. Both opposed meanings are there ready to set off quite divergent readings, a divergence which has already occurred in Germany with some force, before the first stone is dressed (and I-bean welded). *Charles Jenck*

Up view of library with two floors of administration above. Roof garden at top with stone edging around openings. Large external drop blinds to library glazing.

Full frontal up view of administration entrance with the Director's room below the roof garden and below him the window to the Assistant Director's office.

The topping out ceremory

RICHTFEST : Topping Out Ceremony   Stuttgart 12 February 1982

Gentlemen of the Ministry, ladies and gentlemen. This building is the result of an architectural competition and its design has caused controversy - some think it too monumental, though I believe monuments are an essential element in the city - a city without monuments would be no place at all. Others thought that by keeping the old buildings on Eugenstrasse and Urbanstrasse, we would be compromising the design of the new building: but compromise is the essence of architecture, compromise with site, user requirements, cost, technology, etc.; also I thought it important to try and preserve the identity of this corner of Stuttgart, a city which has been so destroyed by war and post-war reconstruction.

Design development was done in London with help from a joint venture teamwork which included Ove Arup and Partners, London

J S and Ulrike Wilke about to give the topping out address

(and I'm glad that David Atling and Cecil Balmond are here today) with Boll and Partners and EDNP of Stuttgart (and I'm pleased that Herr Hettasch and Herr Eser are here). Also we appreciate the help of Brüssau and Gerber (in acoustics) and particularly Messrs Wilkens, Eckenreiter and Bührlen from the Staatliches Hochbauamt and many others who have made their contribution.

Our office in Eugenstrasse has functioned since October 1978 and most of the work is now done in Stuttgart, though we do have German architects in our London office, unfortunately not all as good looking as Ulla, here, who is translating.

The contractors, Arge-Rohbau, have had particular difficulties in constructing this unique shaped buildings, such as, the making of stepped arched windows, the three dimensional cornice, the S-shaped entrance bay window and the funny shaped columns. However, we are very pleased with the quality of work achieved and the fine standard of building - it should last forever.

Incidentally, the funny shaped columns came about as a cost saving - originally there were no columns in the lower level but to reduce the cost of structural spans we put them in - they also enhance space which otherwise might have been empty and bland -cost saving can be architecturally creative. The flared tops take *off centre* loads, and as columns are ideally placed in rooms -they don't always coincide exactly with loads from above - there are other fake columns, there to make symmetry of groupings.

In the process of building in Stuttgart, I have made new friends, in particular Herr Fecker, the architect to the Finance Ministry who it turns out is an expert on wines as well as on architecture, and Dr Peter Beye - the Director of the Gallery, with whom I've had many friendly boxing matches in the model room.

Finally, I would like to say how satisfactory it is for me that this building, designed in 1977, will be completed and finished before the other museums which we designed in 1975 for Düsseldorf and Cologne - architectural competitions which we didn't win and which are still holes in the ground.

Thank you and best wishes for the completion of the work.

James Stirling

The centering of the topping out wreath
The lifting of the topping out wreath

The topping out feast in the Kunsthalle

JS
78

Up view of the theatre arch occurring at the end of the terrace onto
Konrad Adenauerstrasse. A small circular window is to the rehearsal room.
Colour rendered walls are above stonework.

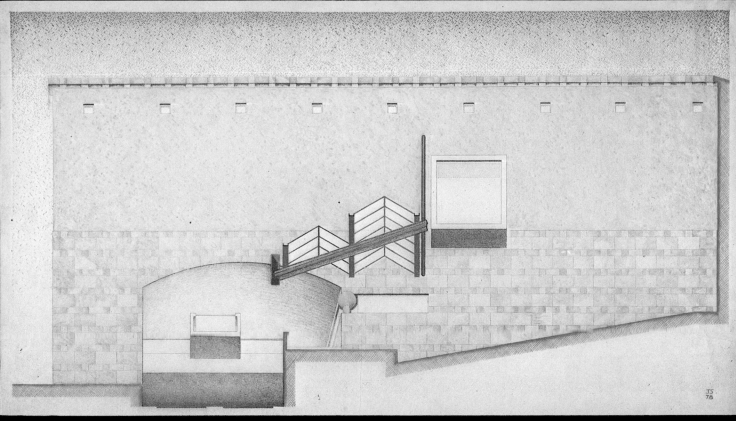

Up view of theatre arch with carpark entrance below. Entrance to the theatre lobby is from under the arch. The glass and steel canopy is over approach steps and window to entrance lobby. The large projecting window is to the theatre foyer which is located between the rehearsal room and auditorium.

Progress photographs, Spring 1982

1978
LUXURY HOUSES
Manhattan New York USA

James Stirling and Michael Wilford

Robert Livesey, Mark Rosenstein

Final street elevation

JS' sketches

The requirement of Sheldon Solow (architect and developer) was for the design of 11 luxury Town Houses (some of which could be apartments), the whole to be 5 storeys high and built over an existing underground parking garage. In anticipation of development above, the garage had included in its roof structure (at ground level) a parallel row of structural beams at 18ft centres to support the party walls of the houses to be built on top. Each dwelling should have its own lift (in addition to staircases) and there should be lavish provision of bathrooms. He hoped that variety in the planning of the houses (and apartments?) could be achieved.

We used the beam spacing to plan an 18ft wide (thin man) house alternating with a 36ft wide (fat man) house, the latter on three lower floors with an independent apartment on the two upper floors; as the lower house was only on three levels it did not contain a lift. With alternating 18ft and 36ft widths we were able to plan three varieties of dwelling. The movement backwards and forwards of the street facade expresses the house within the terrace and the application of bay windows, studio glazing, balconies, etc., indicates the more important spaces within. This is similar to the surface projections - windows, entrances etc., on traditional New York town houses and Brownstones which exist all around the site and give the streets in this area on the upper east side their particular quality. By the design of new buildings we hope to retain the association of wealth and luxury which houses in this high quality residential area undoubtedly have and as these dwellings would be for sale in the luxury residential market they are planned with utmost dollar per square foot utilisation of floor area - there is no vertical space and the planning is quite dense. However the 36ft dimension produces very generous rooms in the lower house and apartments, while the 18ft dwelling benefits from the independence and identity of being a complete house; also the offsetting of its circulation core into the 36ft dwelling allows for large regular shaped rooms. The small front garden set behind railings also is similar to sidewalk and basement areas in this part of New York. The new buildings would be of concrete or steel with external facing of brickwork.   JS/MW & A

60

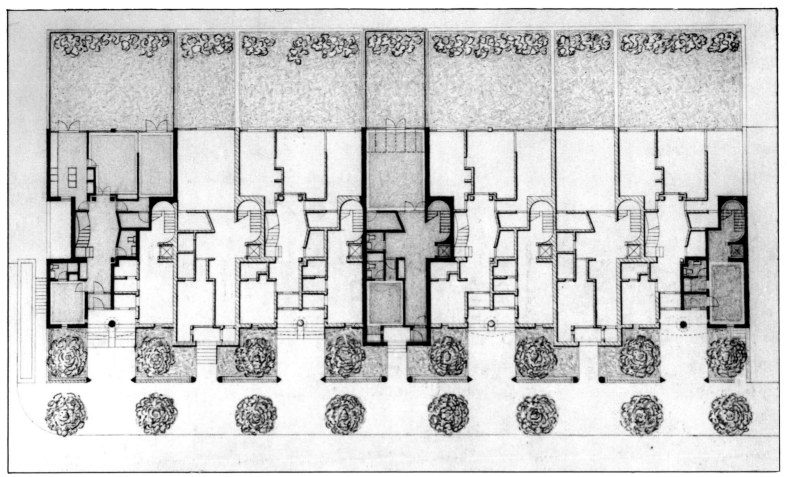

Ground and upper floor level plans

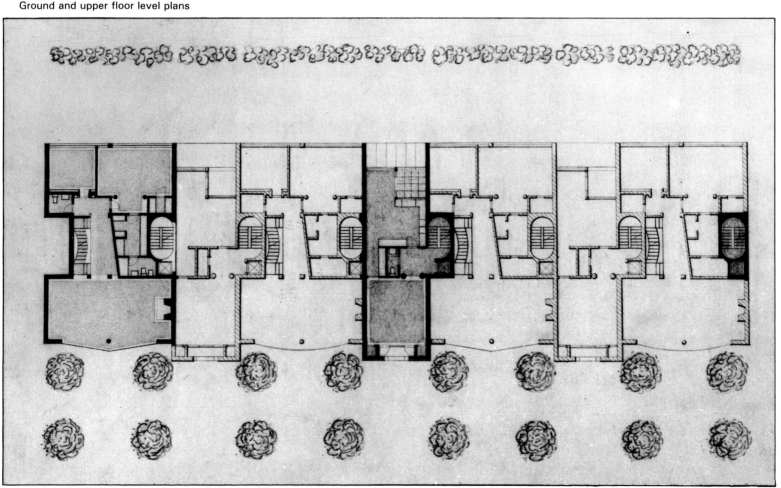

Detail elevation

Sketch elevation

Elevational up view

Cut away axonometric through fat man and thin man apartments

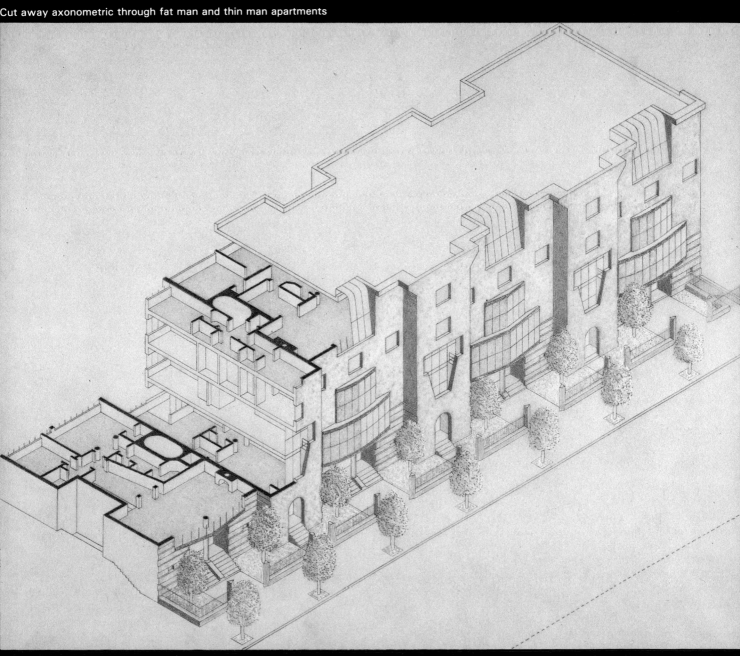

1979
SCIENCE CENTRE
Berlin Germany

James Stirling and Michael Wilford
Peter Schaad, John Tuomey, Walter Naegeli.

The primary need of the Science Centre is for a great multitude of small private offices in which individual and small group work can happen. Conference rooms, directors' rooms, secretaries' rooms, administration offices, etc. are also required. A special concern is how to find an architectural and environmentally distinguished solution from a programme mainly composed of repetitive offices. The *rational* office solution usually produces a banal box-like building. Much of what is wrong with post-war urban redevelopment lies in the uniformity of these rationally produced office blocks and they may be the biggest single factor contributing to the visual destruction of our cities in the post-war reconstruction period.

An additional problem here is the requirement to preserve the facade and larger part of the old Law Courts building (19th century, Beaux Arts and huge in scale) which, due to its central position overlooking the canal, dominates the middle front area of the site. To try to connect new buildings onto the sides of the old building with floor levels of much smaller scale, would visually and practically be extremely difficult and perhaps undesirable as the resulting wall of buildings would tend to *shut off* the interior of the site as seen from Reichspietschufer and the canal promenade. Also a wing of new buildings extending towards Hitzig Allee would compromise the view of the distinguished Shell House which has good exposure as viewed across the empty corner of our site.

Our proposal is to use the three Institutes of the Science Centre (Management, Social and Environment) plus the building for future expansion to create a grouping of three or four *relatively independent* buildings, all of which are similar but different. The architectural form of these buildings may relate to familiar building types and the whole group of buildings, old and new, is perhaps more akin to a College or University precinct. With this proposal, each of the three Institutes could have its own identifying building. Each Institute has two directors with complimentary staff and a dual or binary organisation seems fundamental. As the new buildings are planned from a symmetrical basis, allocation of rooms should adapt to this dual organisation rather well.

However, as each building is connected at every floor level to each other and to the existing building which is used for the Secretariat, they could be occupied in alternative ways — for instance, horizontally, with each Institute occupying one or two floors of all buildings. It was not considered essential to achieve a *close fit* between Institute and particular building and there could be overflow spaces into adjoining buildings.

The new buildings cluster round a central garden of an informal picturesque character and the single large tree in the centre of the site has been preserved. The loggias and arcades which overlook this garden also have a relationship with the cafeteria, the existing building, conference facilities etc. The cafeteria is at garden level in the Management Institute and the

conference facilites are at ground level in the Social Institute. The car park is at basement level in the Environment Institute. Free standing in the garden is the Library tower with a reading room at ground level having views into the garden.

There are two secondary gardens — a *hedge garden* to the west side of the old building, (with shrub planting of geometric form) and a *pergola garden* on the east side. The *hedge garden* is the site for the expansion building which is located in this corner of the site so as not to be disruptive when building operations take place or in any way change the seclusion of the central garden which will be established and protected by the first phase of buildings. The expansion building also is connected at every floor level to the loop of old and new buildings and from it there are views over the canal and towards Shell House. The *pergola garden* in the south east corner of the site is designed so as to provide an alternative entrance for the whole complex, though the main entrance will continue to be through the central door of the old building. The pergola entrance could function as an entrance for staff and be useful at special times such as conferences or on social occasions, such as garden parties, when large numbers of people might have to be handled. This entrance would also be used by the caretaker getting to and from his apartment which is at garden level in the Management Institute.

With this concept of several buildings each of differing form, informally related to gardens and the existing building, we hope to make a friendly, charming, unbureaucratic place — the opposite of an *institutional* environment, even accepting that the functional building programme is for a multitude of offices and the design of a single complex.

JS/MW + A 1979

The existing building

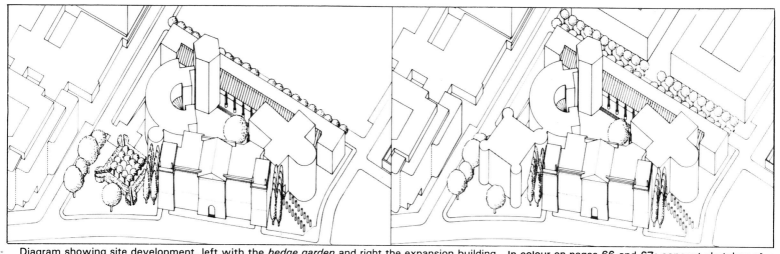

Diagram showing site development, left with the *hedge garden* and right the expansion building

In colour on pages 66 and 67: concept sketches of site development, elevation banding and section

Site plan

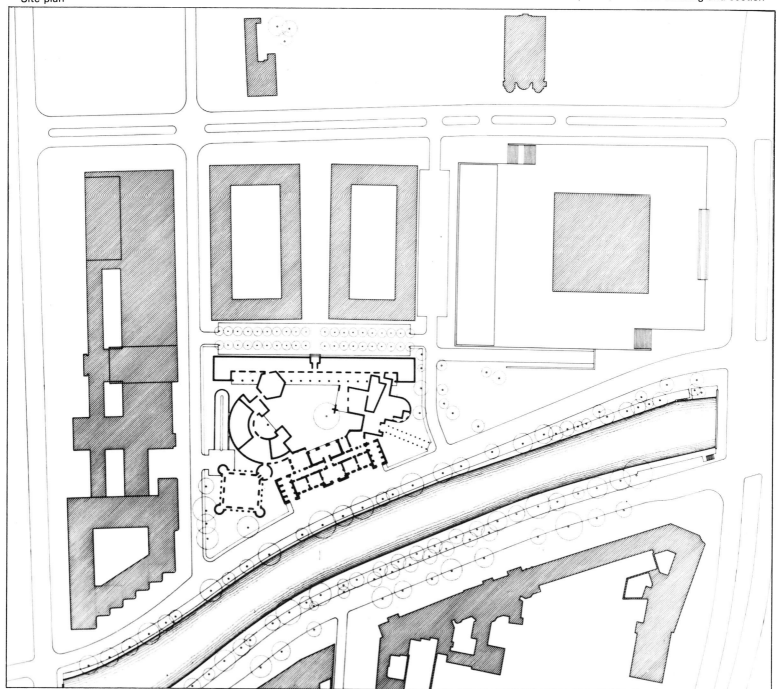

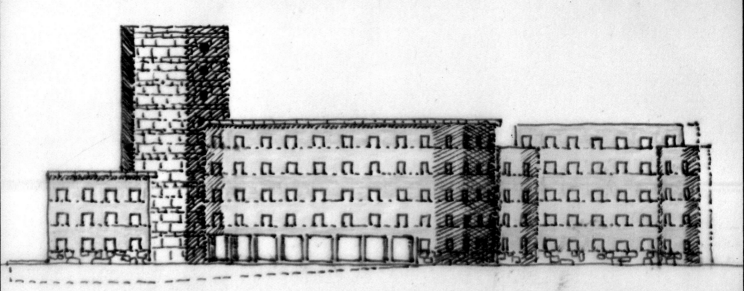

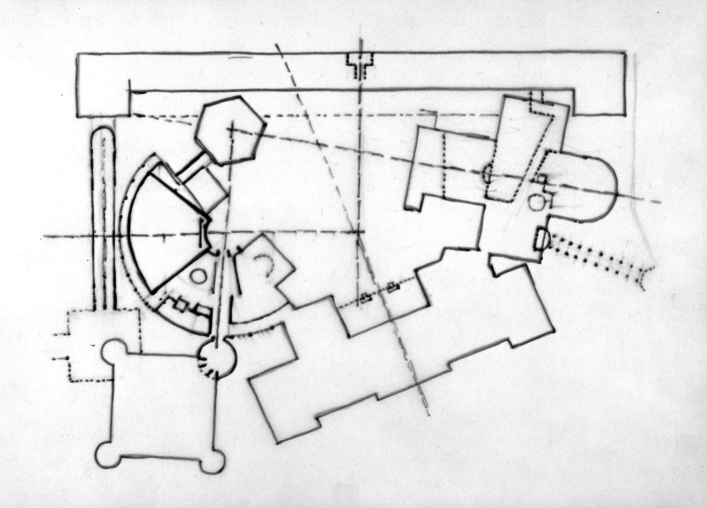

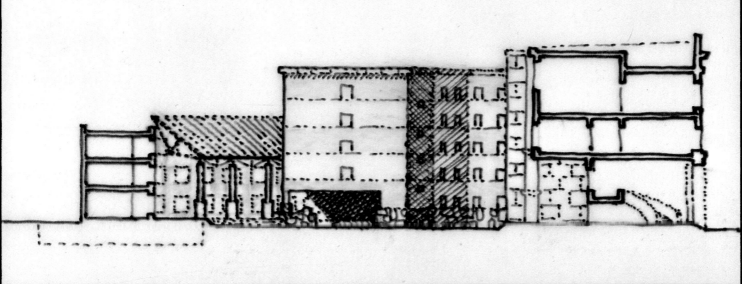

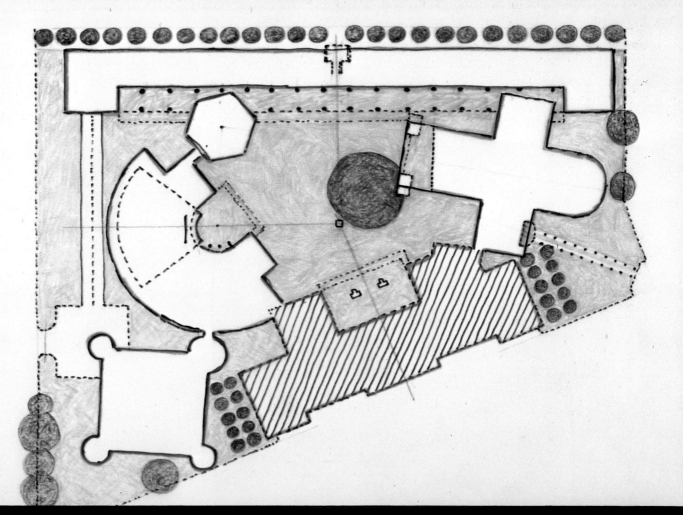

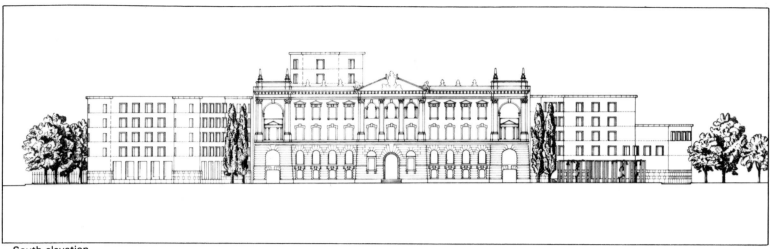

South elevation

Basement plan

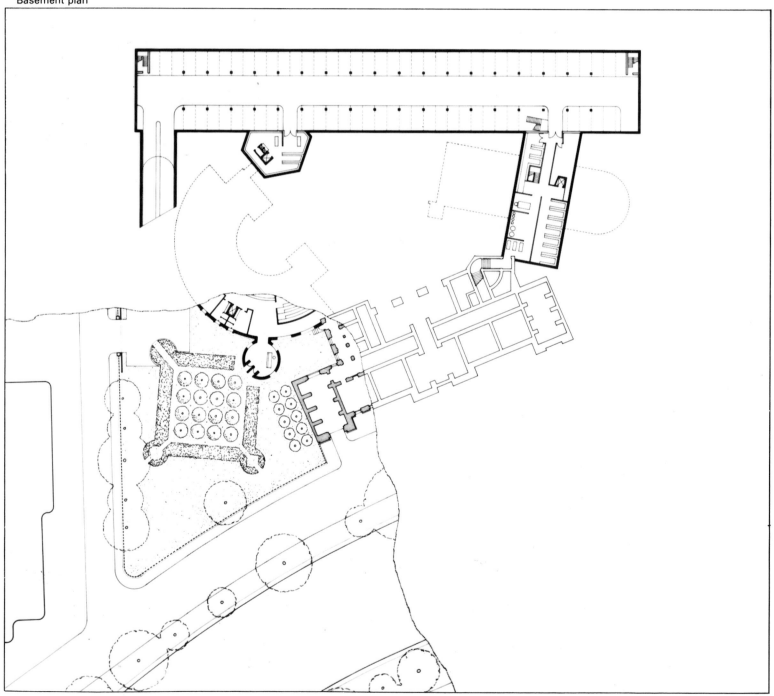

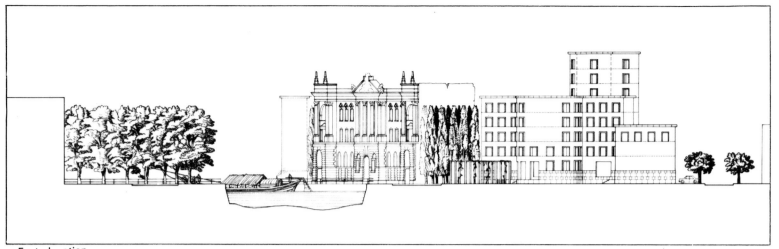

East elevation

Ground floor plan

In colour on pages 70 and 71
Photographs of the model

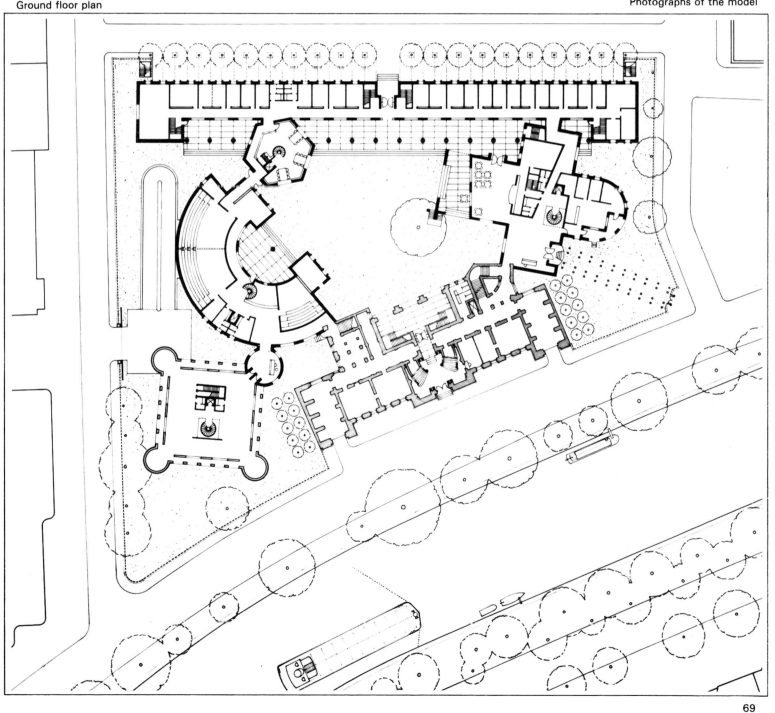

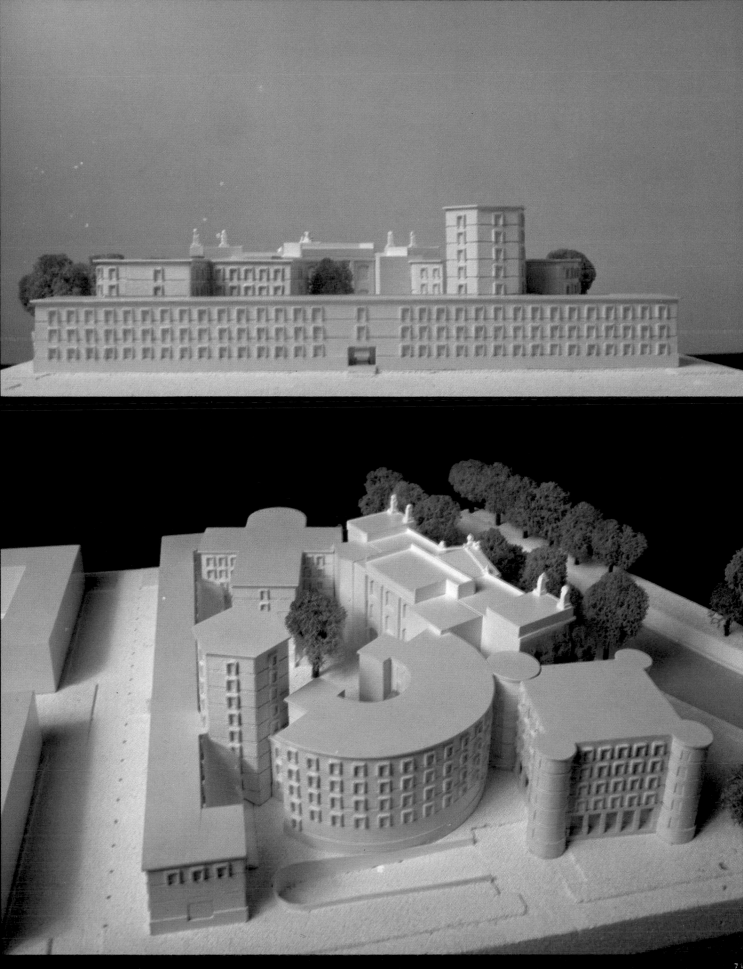

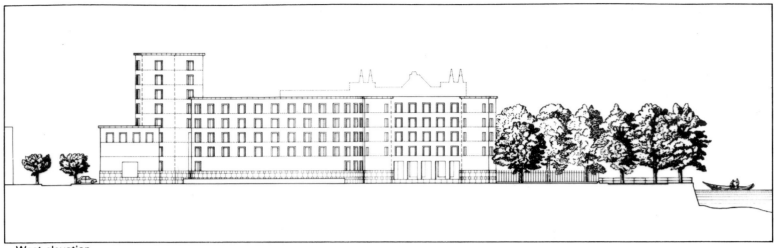

West elevation

Third/fourth floor plan

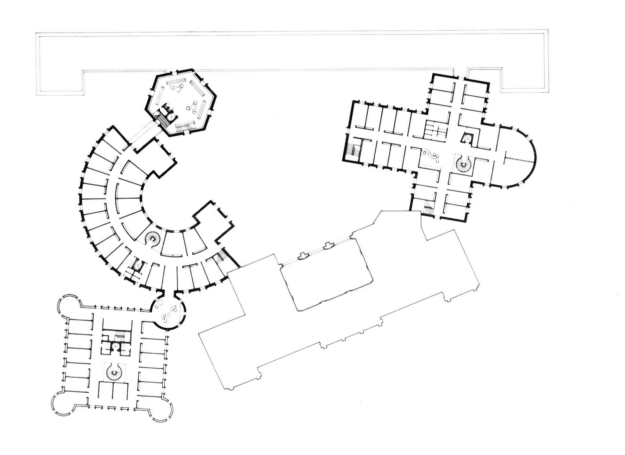

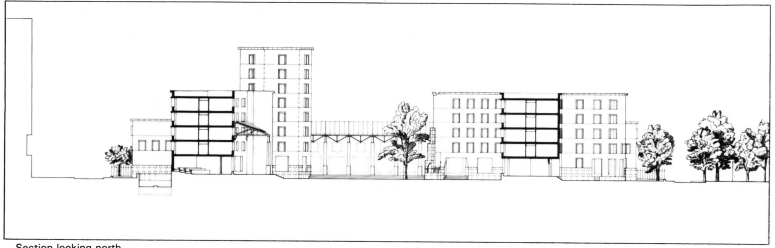

Section looking north

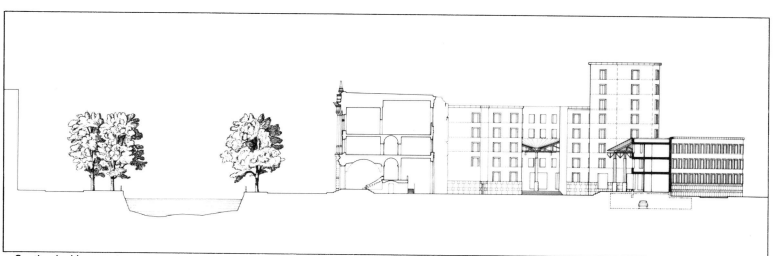

Section looking west

Section looking east

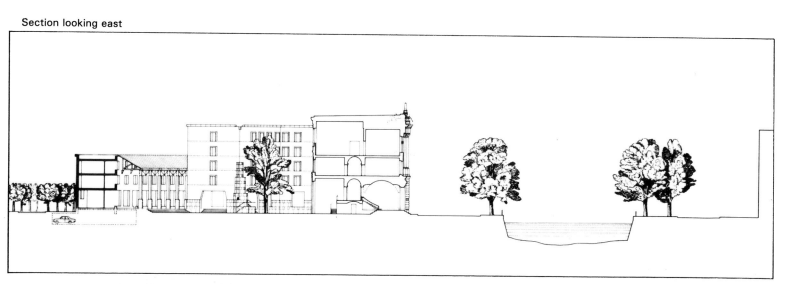

1979
RICE UNIVERSITY
Houston USA

James Stirling and Michael Wilford
Alexis Pontvik and Paul Keogh
In collaboration with Ambrose and McEnany, of Houston

RICE UNIVERSITY SCHOOL OF ARCHITECTURE RENOVATION AND EXPANSION

The new building is L-shaped and interlocks with the North Wing of Anderson Hall to produce a form similar to the Physics Laboratory and Sewall Hall, and consistent with Cram, Goodhue and Ferguson's original strategy of supplementing the narrow buildings of the central quadrangle with linked blocks facing outwards towards the loop road.

The new wing forms a three-sided courtyard with a garden facing west and its open side bordered by the path between Fondren Library and the Chemistry Lecture Hall. The intimate quality of this courtyard contrasts with the central quadrangle and the large green to the west, making a transitional space between them. The proximity of the new building to the Chemistry Laboratory helps define the western end of the area north of the Anderson Hall. Its new relationship with the Physics Laboratory gives an opportunity for the ground area between the two buildings to be landscaped in a character appropriate to its location on a major cross-axis of the campus.

Internally, a spacious double storey circulation gallery and central exhibition/jury space integrates the new wing with the existing building and forms the focus of the School. The gallery is centred on the existing risalit on the courtyard facade of Anderson Hall. The new main entrance is positioned at the north-east corner and opens directly into the gallery, mirroring the existing entrance from the Fondren Library colonnade at the southern end. Internal circulation between the wings of the building occurs through the gallery and exhibition/jury space maximising the informal contact between students, faculty and visitors and encouraging a sense of community in the School. The gallery bridges over the exhibition/jury space at second floor, stopping short of the semi-circular

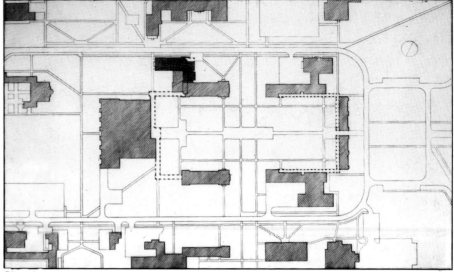
Site plan

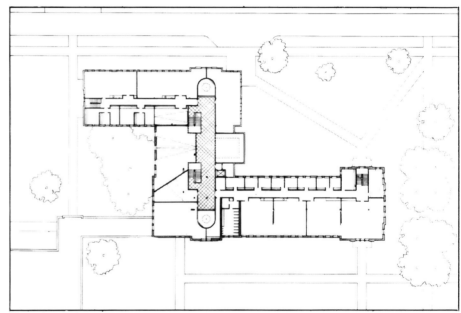
Upper level plan
Lower level plan

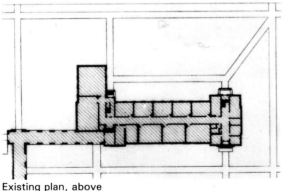
Existing plan, above
alterations and new extension, below

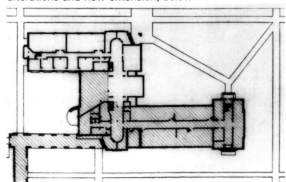

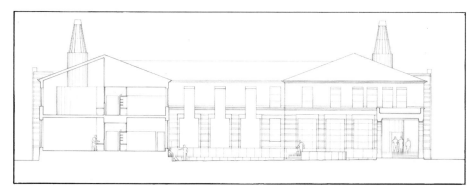

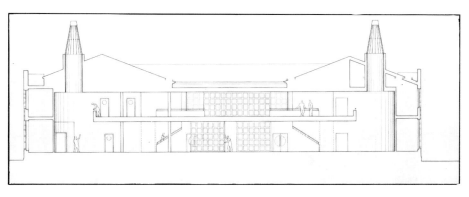

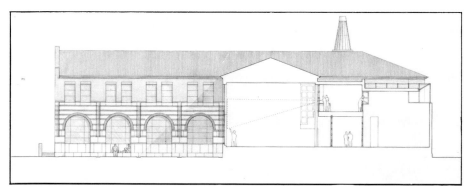

ends to provide visual connection between levels at the entrances. These areas are rooflit by lanterns which also register the terminations of the gallery on the exterior of the building. Staircases connect both gallery levels on either side of the exhibition/jury space.

The exhibition/jury space can easily be adapted for various activities by means of large sliding doors. Enclosed exhibitions or lectures for a seated audience of approximately 200 can be arranged simultaneously with closed or open juries. The combined area can accommodate large open exhibitions and receptions. Glazed doors provide access into the courtyard garden which in fine weather could function as an extension of the exhibition space for receptions, ceremonies and parties. The gallery serves as an information centre for the School with pin-up boards for notices and posters. It can also be used for ad-hoc exhibitions by students and overflow jury space. The bridge acts as a viewing balcony for the activities below and provides additional exhibition space.

The existing trees provide shade for outdoor activities in the new courtyard garden and the ground surface is paved with brick and stone interspersed with shrubs and stone seats. The platform and steps from the exhibition area form the focal point of the garden and provide an informal stage and seating area.

The variety of shape and size of studios should give each space a specific identity. In order to facilitate efficient use of space by matching student group to studio size each semester and to allow different relationships between students of varying age and experience, studios have not been allocated to particular undergraduate or graduate groups. The second floor corridor in the existing building has been repositioned in order to make better proportioned studio spaces. Individual work stations can be arranged around a group meeting area with pin-up/blackboard adjacent to the entrances. Studios are self-contained and separated from circulation areas for security and acoustic privacy. Shoulder height glazing in partitions provides natural light in the corridor and allows views into and between studios.

The student lounge is adjacent to the Fondren colonnade and has direct access into the new garden.

The Administrative offices are positioned in the new wing adjacent to the main entrance and photographic and computer areas are located at third floor level in the existing building.

The design of the new facades maintains sympathy for the existing campus style. The treatment of masonry and window openings makes reference back to the style of Cram, Goodhue and Ferguson's original buildings. The existing eaves line, primary string and shiner courses are carried through the facades of the new building and it is intended to match as far as possible the facing brickwork, stone trim and clay pantiles.

The first floor of the south facade is articulated with stone panels containing large arched windows reflecting the openings and materials of the colonnade between Anderson Hall and Fondren Library. The second floor windows match the size and proportion of the upper windows in the existing building. The wall surfaces and window openings of the north facade are treated in a similar manner but with brick panels at first floor level and the gallery expressed by a risalit similar in form to that on the courtyard facade. JS/MW & A

Existing buildings by Cram, Goodhue and Ferguson

BUILDINGS IN CONTEXT

PAUL GOLDBERGER

For some years now, architects have been expressing concern for the way in which a new building relates to its surroundings. Whereas modern buildings once tended to be conceived as pure, abstract objects, independent of what was beside them, there is now much more attention paid to the notion of fitting a building into its architectural context - trying, in other words, to make certain that the building echoes many of the architectural themes of its neighbours. It is a philosophy of design that suggests, by implication at least, that it may be better to be discreet than to be original.

Perhaps the ultimate example of such contextual architecture has now been completed here, in this city of generally large and very uncontextual buildings. It is the new building of the School of Architecture at Rice University, and it is the first American work to be completed by James Stirling, the British architect who was the 1981 recipient of the Pritzker Prize, the $100,000 international architectural award that has come to be one of architecture's most significant honours.

Mr. Stirling's reputation, made large by his sleek buildings of glass and brick in England and larger still by his anticipated structures on the campuses of Columbia and Harvard Universities, will lead most observers to expect something other than what he has produced in Houston. The new and fairly modest Rice building is as contextual as architecture can be - its facades virtually reproduce the elements making up the exterior of the old architecture building to which it is joined. It is, save for certain details, an almost direct imitation of the older buildings of the Rice campus.

Now, this is not a normal debut at all - one of the most eminent architects in the world, trying his hand for the first time in the United States, doing nothing but imitating the older building next door? What could be going on here?

But this building, while it may shock and dismay those who have seen in Mr. Stirling some sort of answer to the current trend back toward re-use of historical forms - a trend which he has now

joined with a vengeance, despite the different priorities of his earlier work - is in fact a far more thoughtful work of architecture than it first appears to be. It is, in fact, both original and joyful, and it is difficult to spend any significant amount of time in the building and on the Rice campus and believe that Mr. Stirling should have done much of anything else.

A Curious Mix

Rice's main buildings were designed in the 1920s by Ralph Adams Cram, one of the great eclectic architects of the early 20th century, in a style that seems a curious mix of Romanesque and Spanish mission architecture. The university has required that all later building use a pale orange brick and limestone details to conform to the Cram buildings, and although it has not required that Cram's ornate detailing or even his hybrid style be repeated, it has demanded a certain sense of continuity.

In some of the buildings, this is successful; in others, less so. It was Mr. Stirling's wisdom to realise, as few other architects who have worked on the Rice campus in recent years have done, that the buildings which sought originality the most have been the ones that succeeded the least. So this is, if nothing else, a lesson in restraint - a reminder that one sign of great talent is the knowledge of when to hold back, a reminder that hubris is not always the solution in architecture.

Quirky, Warm, Affectionate

But to leave it at that would be to sell this building short. The fact of that matter is that Mr. Stirling was hardly doing nothing, or literally reproducing the older buildings of Rice. His new architecture school is full of subtle variations, of tiny changes which show the presence of his hand. It is a work that provides immense visual pleasure - it is quirky and warm and affectionate, taking the older building's themes and giving them a kind of life that they never before had.

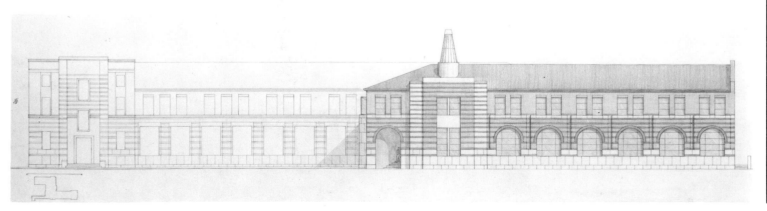

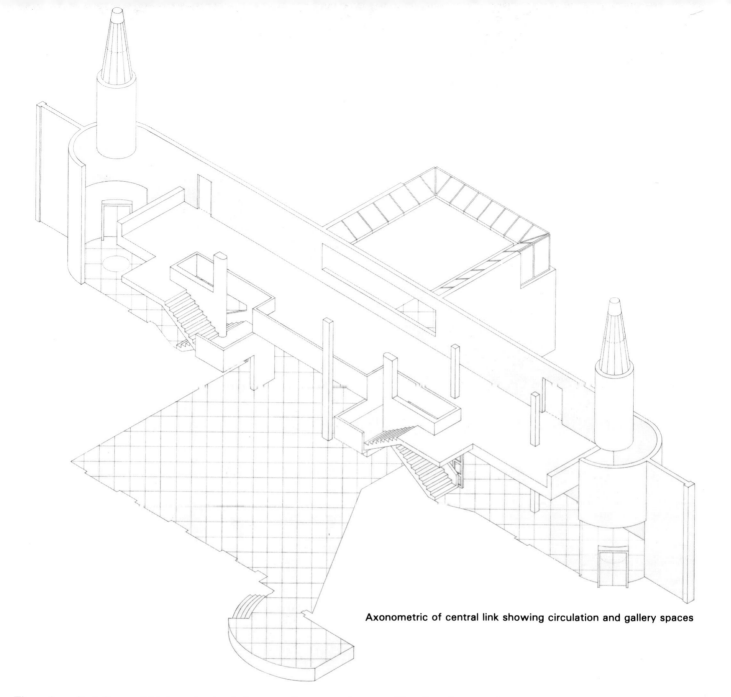

Axonometric of central link showing circulation and gallery spaces

There is a first floor of high arched windows and a second floor of square ones, and there is limestone trim within which are set stripes of orange brick - all details that come from Rice's older buildings, but here composed and arranged in Mr. Stirling's own way. The facade that is most eccentric is at the far end of this L-shaped building; it is of orange brick, with a two-storey arch within which is set a round window off centre. At the base is a doorway bisected by a column and at the top are lines of brick serving as ornament. None of this is without purpose, though the column in the midst of the doorway is mannerism gone a bit perverse. But the overall form of this facade gracefully and subtly echoes the arches of a lovely little building just across the road from this one.

Within the L-shape that the building's plan takes, Mr. Stirling has created a pleasant garden court, like many of the aspects of this building something that one might think had been there for a generation. But once again, the goal is not to create a sustained illusion - there are curious cone-shaped skylight towers, like little rockets, on the roof, and the entrances are through round bays of glass, all of which make it clear that this is not a building constructed in the 1920s. But these details never take over and control the building - the central idea is the continuity with what has come before.

The interior consists mainly of pleasant, matter-of-fact drafting rooms, unfortunately with all-too-institutional lighting. There is a two-storey central space which is used as a display gallery, but that is the only interior area that has any aspirations toward monumentality. The rooms are comfortable and logical without being insistent, and interesting without being shrill.

It is no surprise that the building is fairly popular with students - it is far pleasanter to be in than most architectural schools, and indeed, in its restraint it offers a lesson that most buildings in which architecture is taught eschew. Mr. Stirling's building at Rice is, in a sense, as far as we could come from Paul Rudolph's epoch-making Arts and Architecture Building at Yale of 1963, the monumental concrete structure that summed up the heroic aspirations of a generation, and in its modernity was in deliberate and complete contrast to the Gothic architecture of the rest of the Yale campus.

But of course both buildings seek to teach architecture by example. At Yale, the example was grand and sweeping and dogmatic; it evoked both great admiration and great anguish in those who came in contact with it. At Rice, the example is modest and restrained and altogether discreet. It will be interesting to see what effect Mr. Stirling's lesson has on the teaching of architecture in Houston.

1979–84
FOGG ART MUSEUM
NEW BUILDING
Harvard University USA

James Stirling, Michael Wilford and Associates
Associate Ulrich Schaad
In collaboration with Perry, Dean, Stahl & Rogers

Facade studies

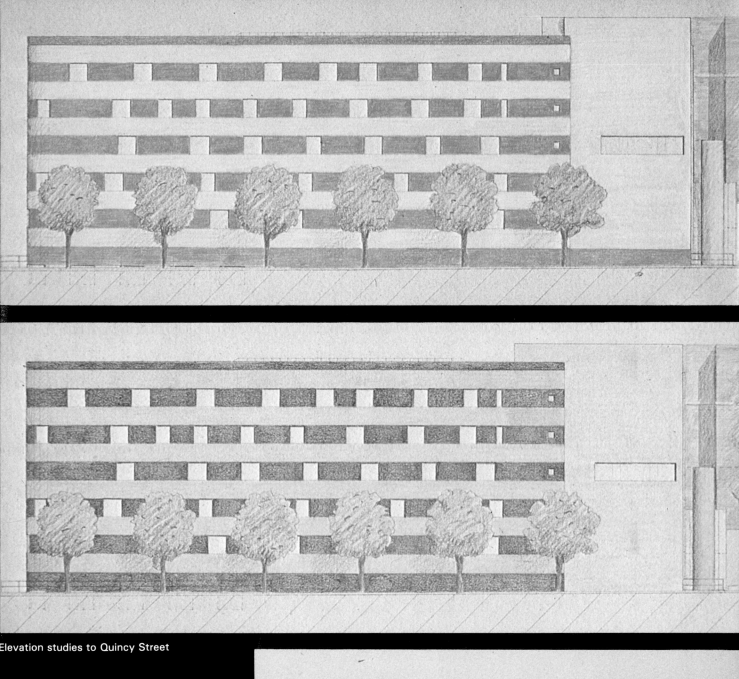

Elevation studies to Quincy Street

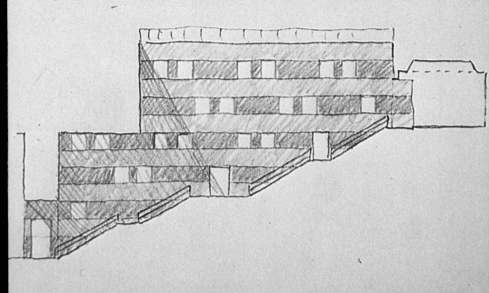

Study for the flank wall of the main staircase

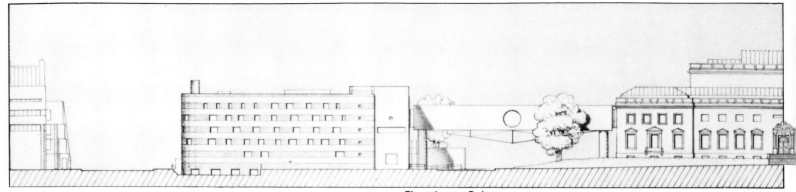

Elevation to Quincy

The new facilities planned for the Fogg Art Museum will occupy an L-shaped site across Broadway from the present Fogg Museum building. Two Harvard-owned buildings – Allston Burr Lecture Hall, an undergraduate science facility no longer needed by the University and a vacant frame house on Cambridge Street – will be demolished to make room for the new structure.

The new building will add more than 38,000 sq.ft to the Fogg's facilities. It will house the Museum's notable collections of oriental, ancient, and Islamic art, and provide much-needed new space for special exhibitions, offices, curatorial and service departments, storage, classrooms, and library collections. Nearly 11,000 sq.ft of exhibition galleries will be created, an increase of more than 75% over the gallery area of the existing Fogg.

The principal facade of the new building will be on Broadway, facing the north wing of the present Fogg. The main entrance, centered in this facade, will be marked by a glass entrance lobby and two monumental functional columns, set into a paved forecourt.

A continuous brick facade, polychromed to reflect the polychromy of nearby Memorial Hall, runs along Quincy Street and curves at the corner to continue down Cambridge Street. Windows are placed functionally, according to the requirements of the rooms.

The new building will be one of the largest facilities at Harvard open to the public on a regular basis. It will contain a large public lecture hall, ceremonial spaces, and galleries both for temporary exhibitions and for the Fogg's permanent collections of oriental, near eastern, and ancient art.

Visitors to the new building will enter from Broadway, through a glass lobby, into a formal entrance hall. Stairs at either side of the entrance hall will lead to a lecture hall on the lower level. A monumental, skylit staircase will rise through the centre of the building to all gallery levels. Its walls will be polychromed in harmony with the exterior. To the left of the stair will be the five office levels of the building, while to the right will be three levels of public galleries. Architectural fragments from the Fogg's collections will be mounted on the walls of the staircase.

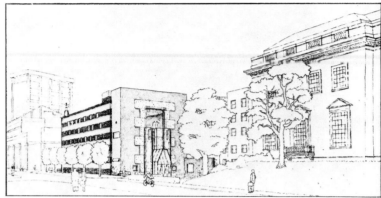

Quincy perspective looking from the existing building towards the new

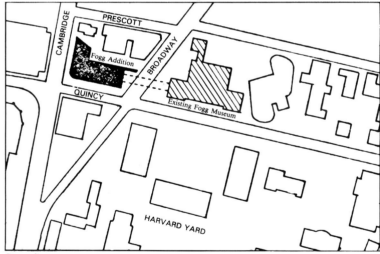

Site plan
Gallery level plan

Entrance level plan

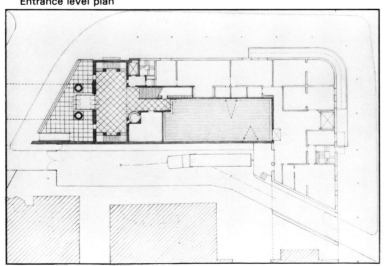

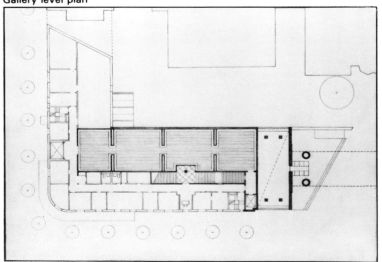

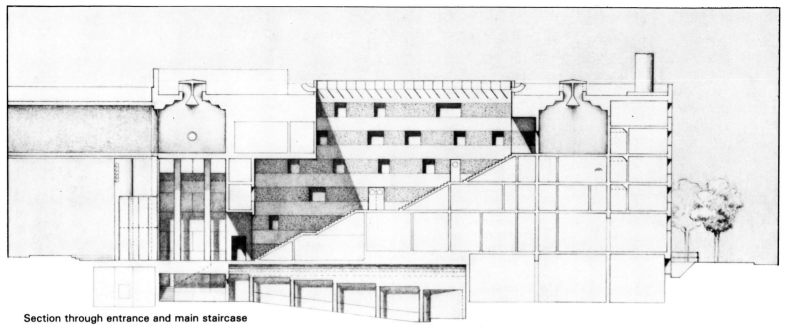

Section through entrance and main staircase

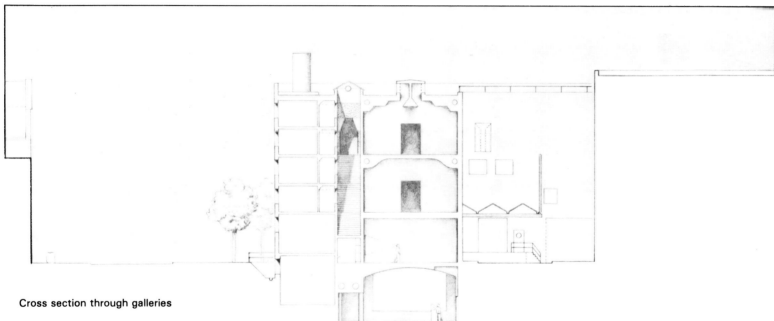

Cross section through galleries

Cross section through entrance and stairs down to lecture hall

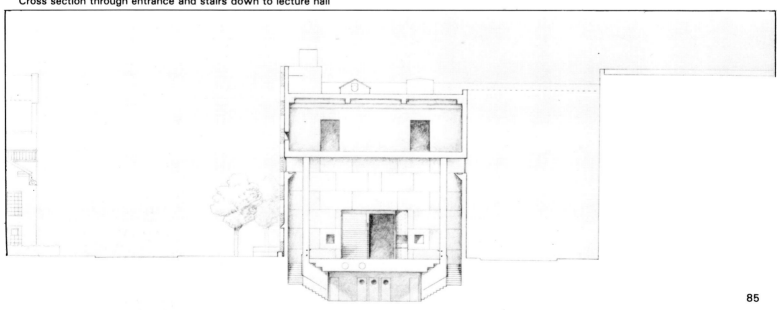

Daylighting study – sunny day

Daylighting study – evening

Entrance hall studies (1)

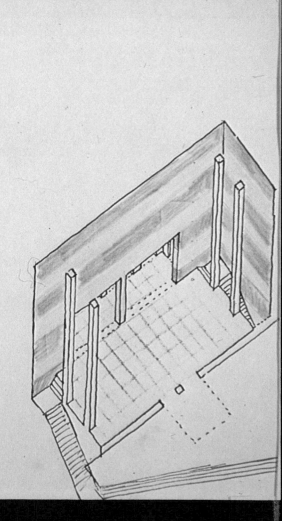

Lecture hall

Entrance hall studies (2)

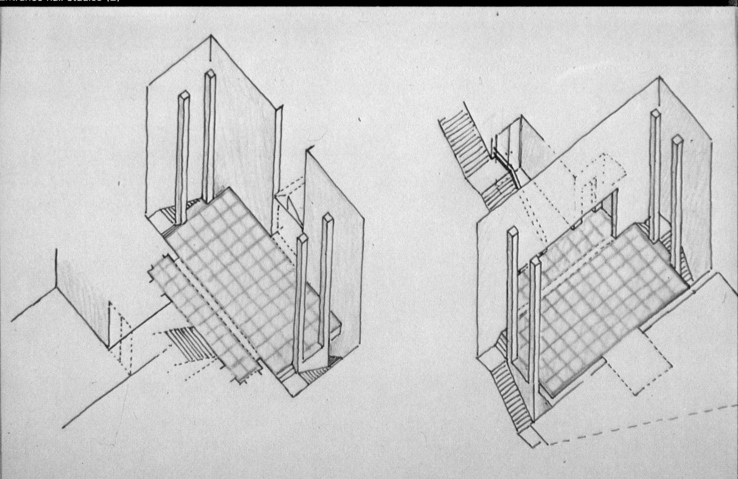

A STYLE CRYSTALLISED

ADA LOUISE HUXTABLE

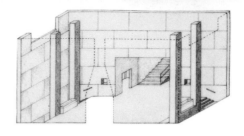

Entrance and hall studies

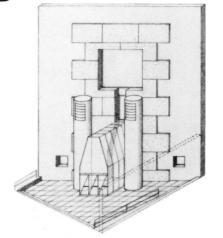

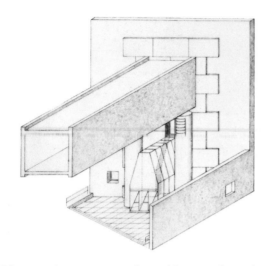

The creative processes in architecture have less to do with the muses of inspiration than with the painstaking resolution of site, programme, structure and plan. That procedure can be understood fairly easily; what is less clear are the aesthetic and cultural impulses that account for those very personal decisions that give the solution its specific shape and style.

The Fogg Museum expansion is the architectural event of the 1980s, which parallels Le Corbusier's Carpenter Hall as the architectural event of the 1960s. A great, gray concrete presence that bursts from its site near the Fogg with monumental exuberance, the Carpenter Center represented the arrival on American, or Harvard soil of the work of one of the great architectural talents of the 20th century.

There are those who see the British architect, James Stirling, as a member of that same exalted company. Now 55, and the recipient of this year's $100,000 Pritzker Prize for outstanding architectural achievement, his firm of James Stirling, Michael Wilford & Associates has three commissions under way in this country - an addition to the School of Architecture at Rice University, a chemistry building for Columbia University and the Fogg, which is being carried out with Perry, Dean, Stahl & Rogers of Boston. Two other projects are nearing completion in Germany.

Stirling has not been a prolific builder, but structures like the Engineering School at Leicester University and the History Faculty Building at Cambridge, in England, are already viewed as landmarks that have had notable international repercussions. Some of this earlier work is as remarkable for the functional flaws of its experimental structure as for its much-copied stylistic trademarks. A high priest of high tech in the 1950s and 60s, Stirling has moved on to explore historical and classical sources in a radically personal way that would set academicians spinning in their Beaux Arts tombs. With his switch from less-than-tried-and-true technology to more traditional methods and materials in recent years, the buildings seem to be holding together much better.

Today's innovators are a more numerous and diversified group than they were in the High Modern period; introspective rather than heroic and universal in their ambitions, they are moving closer to a human scale and context. The new work is not only literary and eclectic, it is often obscure and puzzling in its use of symbols and historical references. It favours image, style and language over social and structural concerns. Nothing could be more instructive about these changes in architectural theory and practice than the

two Harvard buildings. When the Fogg is completed, the dissertations will flower.

With hindsight, it becomes obvious that this has been a steady, ongoing, evolutionary transformation. It is also evident that the changes have crystallised into a new architectural style. Call it an attack, or merely an advance, but what is on the line now is the kind of Modernism in which an abstract concept of geometric beauty was reduced to its simplest visual and structural terms, carefully detached from the traditions and restrictions of the past. It was an architecture that made a bold, revolutionary statement about art, technology and the perfectability of the world. We have become a sadder and wiser society. But even the miscalculations of Modernism are impressive.

The fact is that life and art tend to be messy and lacking in moral consistency. This is a truism that turns out to have certain architectural virtues, as Robert Venturi has reminded us, since the mess is a rich accumulation of cultural acts and accidents. The espousal of messiness, under the names of inclusiveness and complexity, has followed. But what has also followed is that the architect still creates order, by the very process that organises and resolves the problem and its parts. Show me ad hoc architecture by an architect and I will show you relationships that may be subliminal or subversive, but they are there. Or it is not architecture - but that is a serious matter for another time.

James Stirling has dealt in a very high kind of order and organisation in the design of the Fogg; this is a dense, tight plan on a small restricted site that brilliantly solves administrative and gallery needs. The building is remarkable for the creative virtuosity with which its functions are accommodated while suggesting a monumentality that belies actual dimensions. Stirling was lucky to have as a client the director of the Fogg, Seymour Slive, who understood this achievement immediately. Professors John Coolidge and Neil Levine, who arranged the show of drawings that trace the evolution of the project, complete a formidable triumvirate fo sympathetic experts.

But if there is functional clarity here, there is also a great deal of aesthetic complexity. Stirling's current preoccupation is with oddly scaled and strangely evocative elements of archaic and classical periods, with fragmentary historical references wrought large and mysterious; he displays an attachment to the tomb and the crypt and the monuments of the distant past. But he has not lost his infatuation with the trappings of technology. In fact, he has put the two together for an extraordinary classical-technological eclecticism that creates a startling imagery. The classical elements are deliberately distorted and stripped of their original structural rationale to create ironic, surreal and unsettling effects. The results are not easy to forget.

The entrance facade of the new Fogg building is just such an image. The entry itself is a slant-sided, flat-topped enclosure of glass and metal, flanked by two cooling towers like a pair of space-age classical columns. This high tech element is framed by overscaled classical quoins that surround the doors and an opening just above, which may or may not be used for a connecting bridge to the older building. The quoins are to be executed in stone or stucco; their symbolism counts more than any structural connotations.

The small entrance space is expanded vertically with a high ceiling emphasised by false columns, which are used purely as a scaling device. The verticality is further stressed by a central stair on a direct line with the entrance, which rises the building's full height and will be flooded with light from a skylight at the top.

The scheme is best appreciated in section, because the stair is the spine between offices and galleries that provides processional space; it is tightly flanked by five floors of offices on one side and three double-height galleries on the other, separated by a polychrome wall. The offices are random sizes, reflecting staff preferences and needs. Stirling ignored the accepted modernist practice of establishing a modular facade for a formal street elevation. Instead, he has matched random windows to the random offices. Then, with some fast brickwork, he contained the irregular window pattern within polychrome bands, to unify the openings in a horizontal composition that totally transforms the facade's emphasis and balance.

Look carefully, and it becomes evident that those bands are meant to suggest the polychromy of Harvard's most notorious architectural fruitcake, the High Victorian Memorial Hall that is one of the Fogg's near neighbours. Look again, and those horizontal bands pick up the projecting levels of the High Modern Gund Hall just beyond. But this is no modest act of deference to a neighbourhood that is commonly considered an architectural zoo; it is simply a way of living with the animals - now known as contextualism.

Nor do these references make Stirling's design any less powerful a statement of his own intentions. Those intentions are to push the senses to the rediscovery of some of the grandest and subtlest tricks in the architect's bag, through the most provocative means and a sure but very private and internal sensibility.

The critic Charles Jencks has characterised Stirling's recent work as an enigmatic and perplexing conjecture on the past. Stirling sees the juxtapositions of the unexpected as 'delightful ambiguity.' He favours an architecture that is 'neither ancient nor modern, primitive nor technological.' What he admires most is 'a free-wheeling constructive manipulation of elements' in the manner of Hawksmoor and Schinkel.

This is not easy architecture. And it is not innocent architecture. It is knowledgeable, worldly, elitist and difficult architecture. The emphasis is on myth and monumentality rather than on the old partnership of form and function. But it is in essential spatial and structural skills, in the total integration of image and purpose, that Stirling and Le Corbusier share common ground. No symbolism or metaphor can substitute for that. Call the new architecture revivalism, revisionism or revolution, the fact remains that you've got to be as good as Stirling to pull it off.

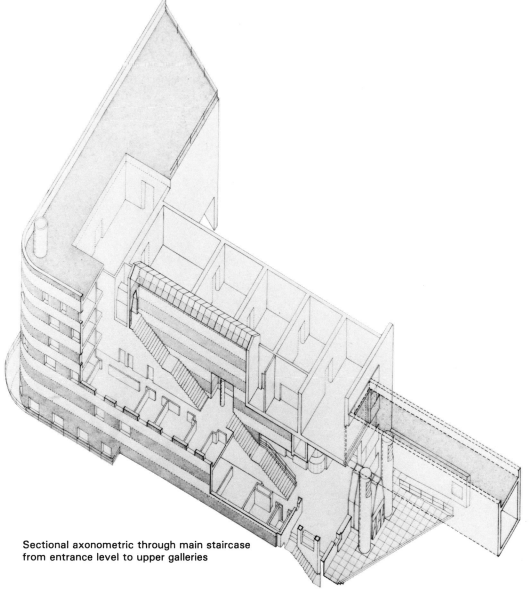

Sectional axonometric through main staircase from entrance level to upper galleries

THE CLORE GALLERY
Turner Museum and Tate Gallery Expansion London

View of model

LITERAL ECLECTICISM
CHARLES JENCKS

Beehive tomb entrance, Mycenae

This extension to the Tate Gallery takes its cues literally from the surrounding context, then modifies them to a subdued, squared-up geometry. From the right side the brick invades the infill panels, from the left side the stonework, cornice and colour of the Tate fills up the panels. The back, for servicing and contrast to the more public front, is very late Bauhaus Modern, just where it ought to be. To make the contrast more piquant, Stirling has run some of the facades around the corners so that they can fight it out on a single wall. The 'dumb' literalness of these contrasts annoys certain critics who, mistakenly, term it 'pastiche', or 'jokey modern' (Colin Amery). Wilful logic it may be, but certainly not jokey. Like Stirling's work of the 1960s, it has an uncompromising bluntness in parts – it doesn't seek to ingratiate – and this quality has raised doubts in the past. Thus it is presumably meant to do so here.

Lutyens' Page Street House, 1930

The building's very simple L-shape has absorbed a variety of elements. Most prominent is the eroded pediment over the revolving door, a juxtaposition of elements that recalls the 'Treasury of Atreus' at Mycenae. The stonework here and 'oddly' proportioned segmental window relate to George Dance's Newgate jail, as well as directly to the Tate's stonework opposite.

To show breaks and transitions Stirling has used several modernist compositional techniques. He ends the infill square bays with a quarter beat and then elides them into the next theme; or he suddenly cuts them away abruptly, thus providing the typical Late-Modern 'non joint/joint' – a rhetorical figure that Isozaki has perfected. Indeed the main, voided pediment is an example of the cut-out approach; one that is unthinkable with Neoclassicism or any of the Classicisms save Free-Style.

A clear separation of surfaces to accentuate depth and function is allowed by this method. For instance the square glass wall is sunken back twice, at the entrance and corner public reading room, to become a reference plane which unites similar activities – in this case, a view of the garden. The most unusual and therefore controversial aspect of the whole building is the treatment of this

corner. Four odd things happen at once. A funny window pivots out (shades of Breuer's Whitney Museum?). The brick infill steps up to the right and then suddenly jumps over space to hang. Brick hanging. The glass wall behind chamfers back to avoid these falling bricks and the entablature quickly changes sex.

As if to tone down this wild set of incidents (and one must remember they all have functional and contextual 'justifications'), Stirling has united them into the lines and volumes of his addition. To object to this picturesque symbolism is to object to a tradition stemming from J C Loudon. Of course it has often produced conventionally ugly buildings, but then they are meant to compensate for their lack of harmony with lots of truthful character. That's what we have here – and it's also a beautiful building in its parts. Several notable things are happening at once. The building purports to be a classical addition to a classical set-piece, but as we've just noted it's a Free-Style Classicism, or one handled with a picturesque surface and an eclectic set of details. If the symmetry is being kept by the Lodge on the river front, right, and its counterpart to the left, then the Stirling addition would call for another compensating one to cut off the left-hand street – if one were

Detail of entrance, model

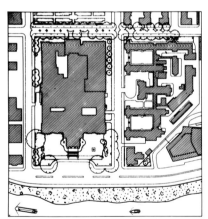

Site plans, before and after extension

Site massing model

following straight classical precedent. This will probably not happen, and it is not in the proposal.

There are several precedents for this asymmetrical symmetry, and Stirling mentions the model of the garden building added to the big country house; but one can still have doubts. From afar the totality will create the impression of a balanced body with one lopsided wing. Closer however, the way most people will experience it, the volumes and surfaces will work in the 'conversation' he mentions. They will respond one entrance to another, one shape and texture to another.

Some of the most interesting aspects concern the sequence of spaces. After we have gone through the Mycenaean pediment and low entrance lobby, the space shoots up in an L-shape (recalling the plan) and focuses through a tall window, in the direction of the galleries on the upper floor. The hollowed-out space is very tight, economic, Mannerist and dramatic – a rectangle which then shifts to the right under a cantilever. Now the erosions of the infill panels and their surrounding quoins really work rhetorically to slice the space, as they themselves are sliced. By running over the volumes, not at the edges as in classical

aesthetics but elsewhere as in Wrightian aesthetics, Stirling can show the square wall pattern as an ordering system, not as substance. Like a Renaissance application of pilasters, this square 'order' is conceptual rather than real structure: the cantilevered pattern makes this clear.

Finally, the culmination of the route, the Turner galleries, is the excuse for the whole design. These are top-lit and indirectly lit with light bouncing off the centre scoops as in Aalto and Kahn's recent museums. In section they may remind us of Roman ovens or medieval kitchens, but as built they will provide an eerie glow of white light that is modulated with sfumato. A single external window, and view of the river, is throughtfully provided for relief from this unremitting experience of art and architecture. After this feast of vintage Turner and Stirling the cultural gourmand will relish it. The beauties of eclecticism are those of flexibility, variety and depth. An eclectic building of Borromini can respond to various opposite buildings in a site, can change character, even mood, with different functions, and relate fully to a complex, cultural past. This the Clore Gallery, the first major cultural commission in London since the National Theatre, will do.

CJ

Up view of rear elevation facing towards Vickers Tower. Louvre controlled
windows to the print collection room and studio glazing (north facing) to
the conservation department at ground level. Glazing canopy over
tailboard level shipping and receiving service entrance.

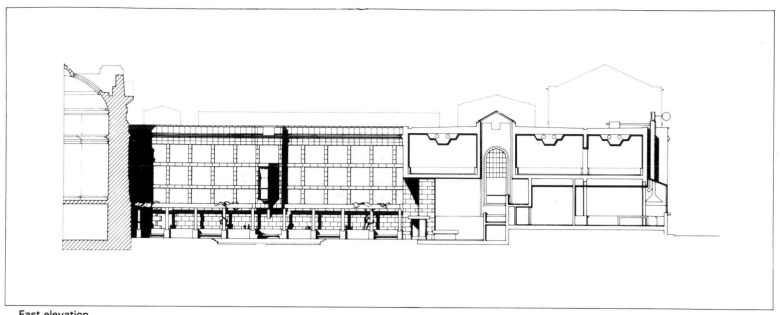

East elevation

South elevation

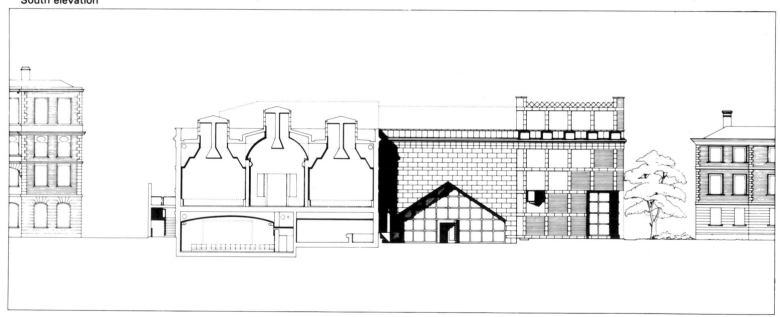

Ground floor plan

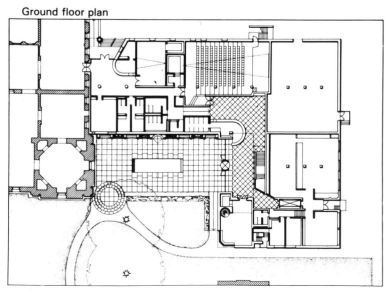

Upper level plan

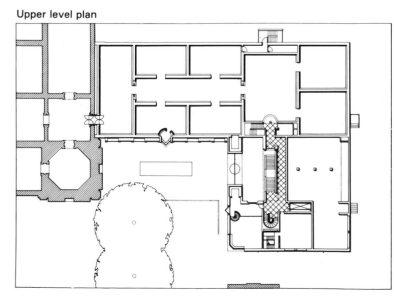

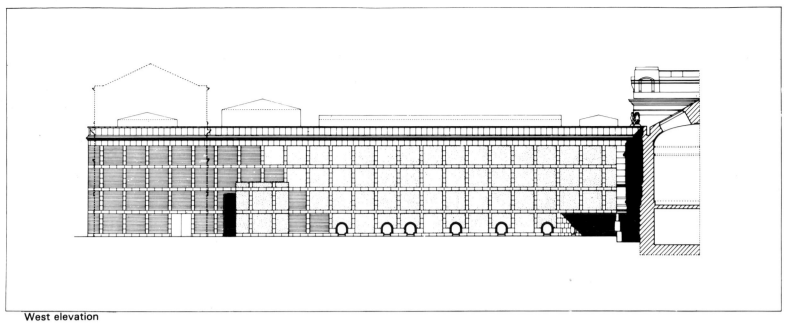

West elevation

North elevation

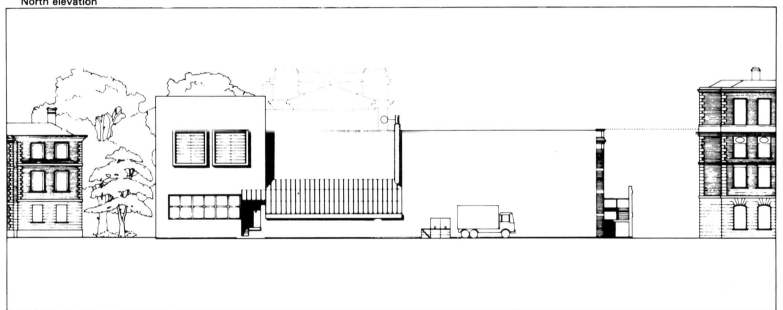

Upper and lower axonometric views of junction with Clore Gallery

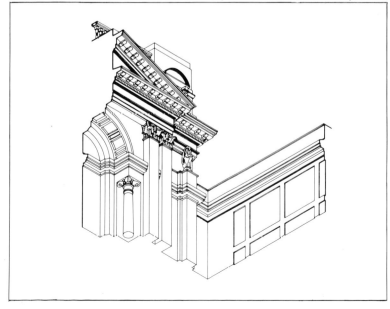

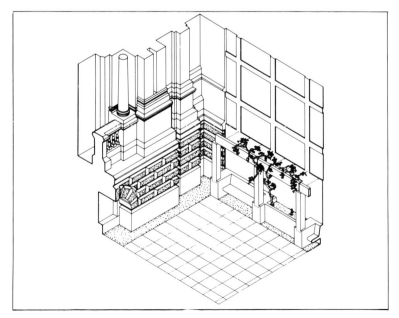

The Clore Gallery for the Turner Collection will be the first element in the development of the Queen Alexandra Hospital Site for use by the Tate Gallery, and it was essential to position the new building in a way that would not inhibit further development. Certain visually important buildings of the Hospital complex are to be retained and integrated with the new building. The Lodge on Bulinga Street/Millbank will be retained. At the moment it is used by the Ministry of Defence and, when available to the Tate, will be ideal for garden functions and tea rooms, with offices and VIP accommodation above. We will also retain the Hospital entrance building on Bulinga Street which may overlook a future sculpture garden and be used as a library/bookshop and for archives. Other remaining Hospital buildings are to be used for offices and storage. The retention of the Lodge with its counterbalancing relationship to the Royal Army Medical College to the south-west preserves the contextual setting of the Tate and maintains the symmetrical balance of the Gallery about its entrance portico. Nevertheless, the Clore Gallery will have its own separate identity and be clearly seen from Millbank across the gardens of the Tate. The existing plane trees will be maintained and new lawns laid across Bulinga Street to the Lodge.

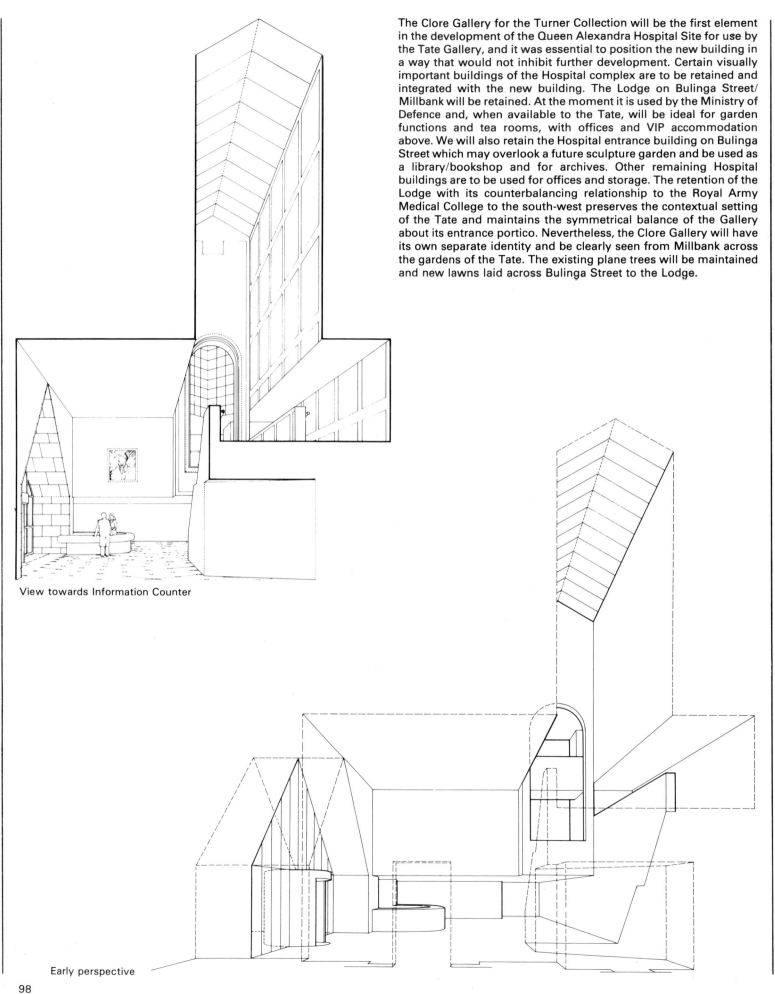

View towards Information Counter

Early perspective

The new building is designed as a garden building (extension to the big house) with pergola and lily pool, a paved terrace with planting and sheltered seating. It will be L-shaped with a gallery wing connecting to the existing building immediately behind its pavilioned corner. The shorter wing returns towards Millbank on the line of the existing Lodge. Setting back the new building and matching its parapet to that of the Tate allows the pavilioned corner, with its greater mass and height, to maintain its architectural significance and leaves the symmetry of the Tate frontage undisturbed.

Approach to the new building will be either from the front steps of the Tate or through a new gate in the garden railings to Millbank and along footpaths to a paved entrance terrace. This sunken terrace relates the corner pavilion with the entrance of the new building and will be a gathering place for visitors and, as it faces south, a good place for sandwich lunches. The increased height of the new building (administration floors) adjacent to the Lodge reinforces the feeling of enclosure at the entrance terrace and complements the pavilion corner of the Tate.

The entrance of the new building does not face towards the river

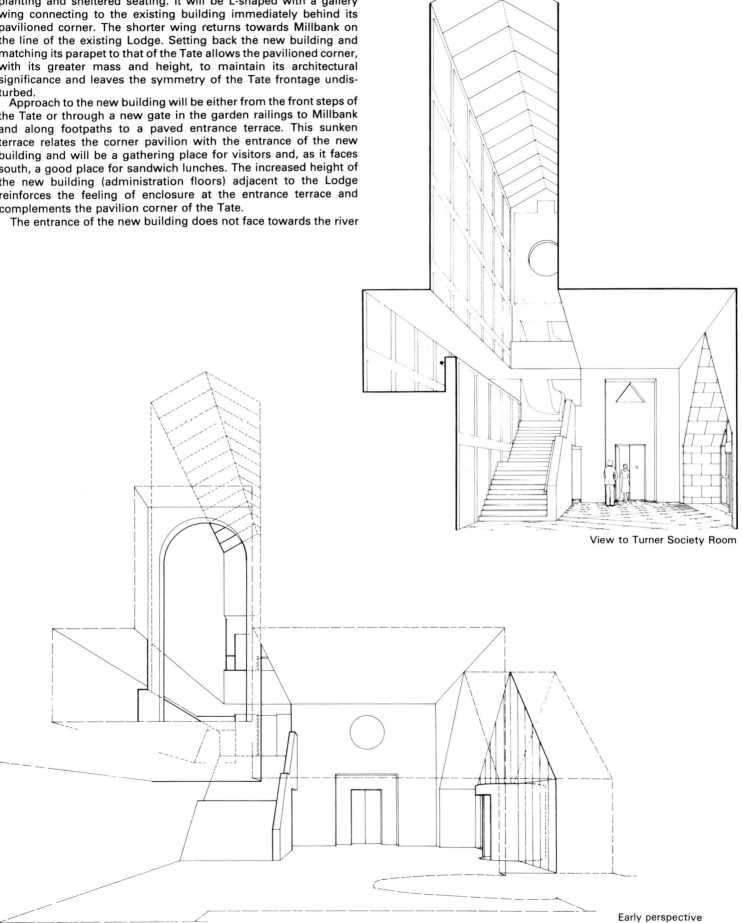

View to Turner Society Room

Early perspective

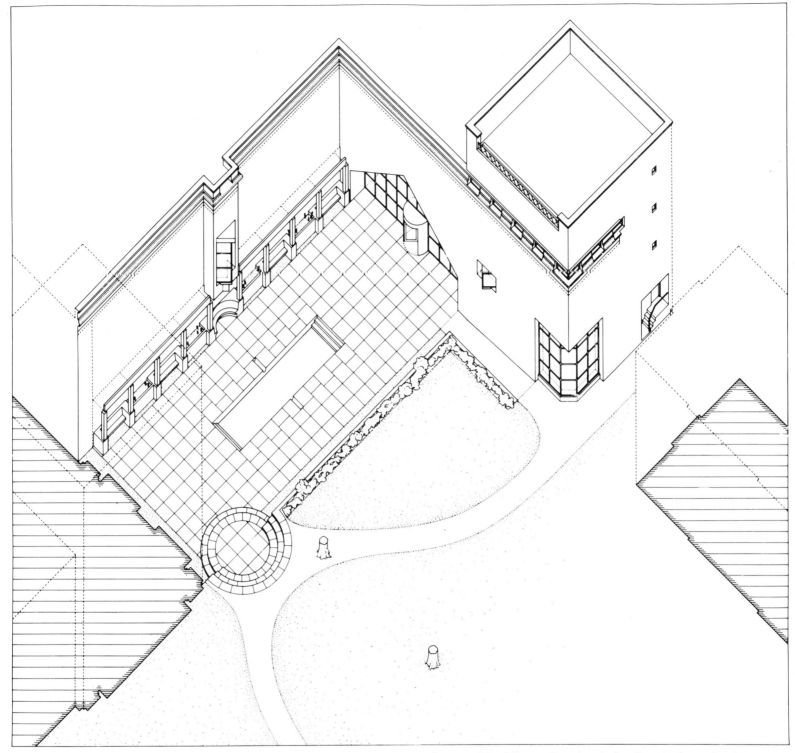

Axonometric of the south and east elevations to the sunken terrace

(avoiding competition with the entrance of the main building), but sideways towards the Tate portico/steps and the shoulder of the Tate – an architectural conversation between the new entrance and the pavilioned corner across the terrace is intended. The existing cornice is carried across the principal facades of the new building and stonework details of the Tate walls are carried partially on to the building. The garden facades have panelling of stone with rendered infill (stucco). Towards the Lodge and Hospital building the panels are infilled with brickwork to match the existing buildings. The colour of rendering will be chosen to mediate between the Tate stonework and the brickwork. The height of the pergola on the terrace relates to the Tate's rusticated base. The secondary facades (NE and SE) are in a light coloured brickwork with coloured metal window elements.

The upper level of the new building contains the galleries and these are at the same level as those in the Tate, allowing uninterrupted flow of visitors to and from the main building. There is a sequence of rooms, smaller and larger, related to the scale and grouping of Turner's pictures. Daylighting will be through roof lanterns. A centrally placed bay window in a small room off one of the galleries is a place to pause, to sit and rest one's feet and enjoy views into the garden and across the river.

Non-exhibition spaces are located at the lower level and include the entrance hall, lecture theatre (180 seats), staff facilities, paper conservation department, plant room, etc. In the entrance hall there is an information and cloaks counter and a showcase containing the Turner relics (his model ships, palettes, glasses, snuff box, etc) as well as the main staircase leading to the galleries. There is also a public reading room overlooking the garden which is fitted with a small servery where drinks and sandwiches can be prepared for

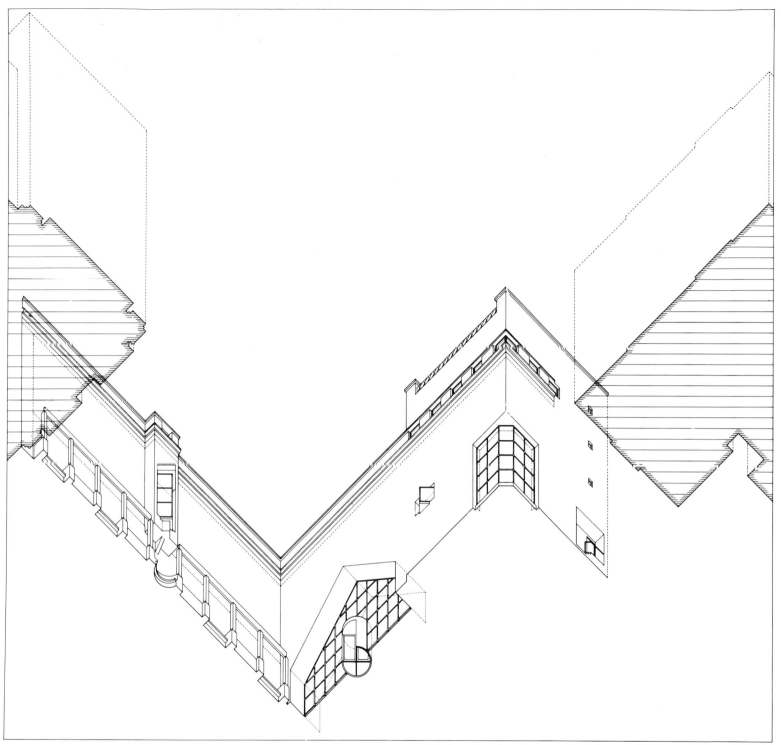

Up view of main entrance and window to the Turner Society Room

evening functions using this room and the adjacent entrance hall, perhaps related to evening lectures. A large lift serves all levels, linking galleries, reserve galleries, print department, paper conservation department, etc; it will carry the largest of Turner's paintings, staff and invalids.

An entrance at the rear of the building serves equally the education facilities in the Tate and those to be provided in the new building (classroom and Lecture Theatre).

As Bulinga Street will be built over only in the area required for the Clore Gallery, the remainder of the street will provide access and parking from John Islip Street. A footpath linking John Islip Street to Millbank will be a continuation of the Bulinga Street pavement through a landscaped area to the north of the new building.

The new building is approximately 3880m². By omitting the paper conservation department, print room and two reserve galleries, it would be possible to build a reduced size of building (approximately 3100m²) if this were financially necessary. The building will cost about £6 million and is scheduled to start on site in early 1982 and be completed in 1984.   JS/MW + A

James Stirling, Michael Wilford & Associates with
Property Services Agency, Museums and Galleries Group
Associate-in-charge: Russel Bevington, Associate: Peter Ray
Assistants: John Cairns, John Cannon, Robert Dye, Lester Haven, Walter Naegeli, Sheila O'Donnell, Philip Smithies, Stephen Wright
Felix J Samuely & Partners, Consultant Structural Engineers
Steensen Varming Mulcahy & Partners, Consultant M & E Engineers
Davis Belfied and Everest, Consultant Quantity Surveyors
John Taylor & Sons, Consultant Public Health Engineers
Janet Jack, Consultant Landscape Architect

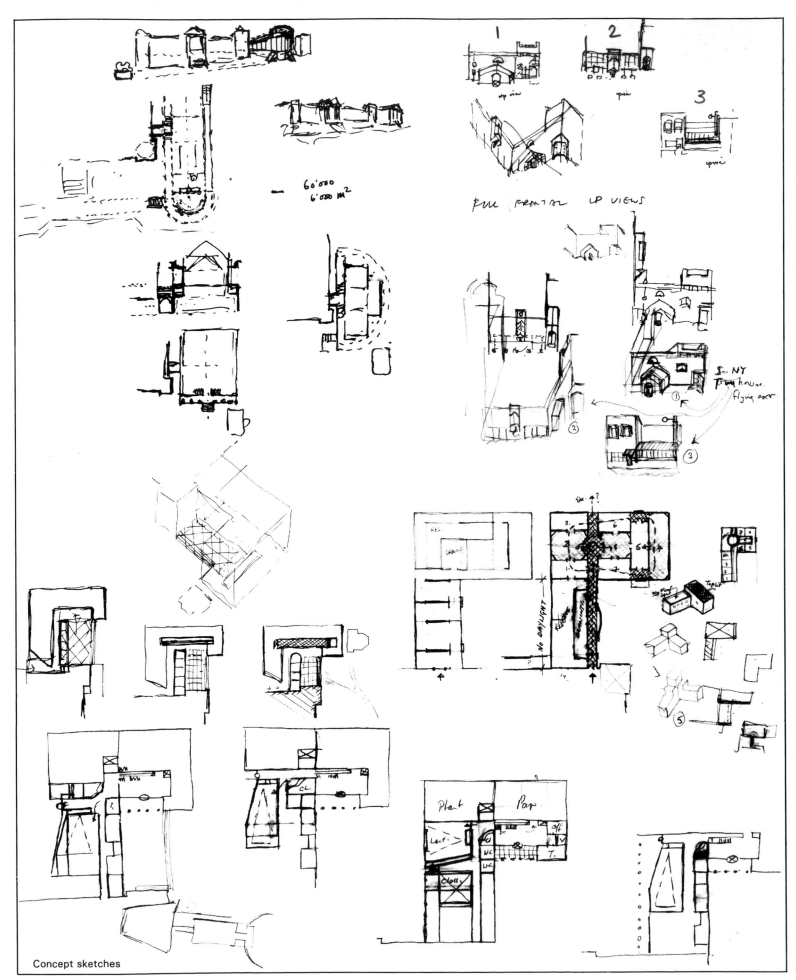

Concept sketches

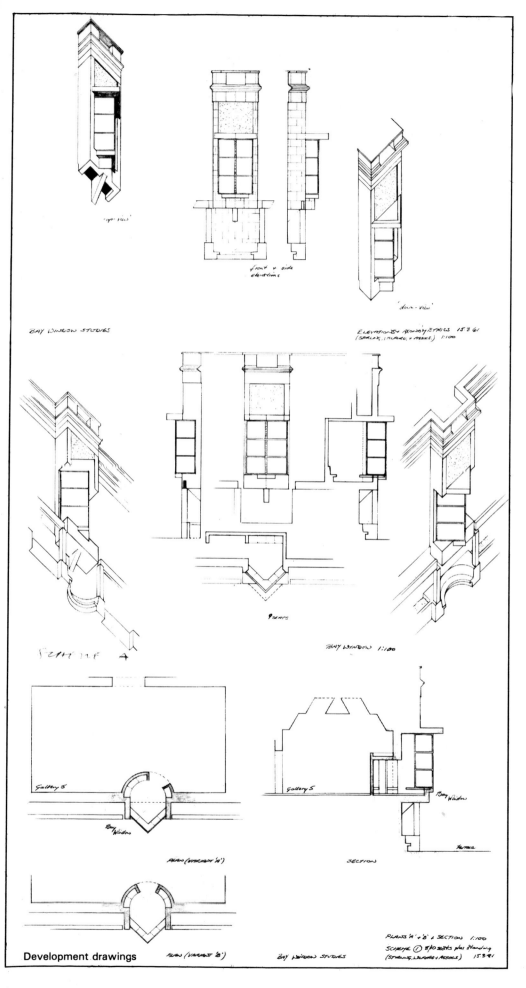

BAY WINDOW STUDIES

ELEVATIONS & AXONOMETRICS 15·3·61
(STIRLING, WILFORD & ASSOCS) 1:100

9 SEATS

BAY WINDOW 1:100

Gallery 5

Gallery 5

Bay Window

Terrace

SECTION

PLAN (VARIANT 'A')

PLAN (VARIANT 'B')

PLANS 'A' & 'B' & SECTION 1:100
SCHEME ① 8/10 SEATS plus standing
(STIRLING, WILFORD & ASSOCS)   15·3·91

BAY WINDOW STUDIES

Development drawings

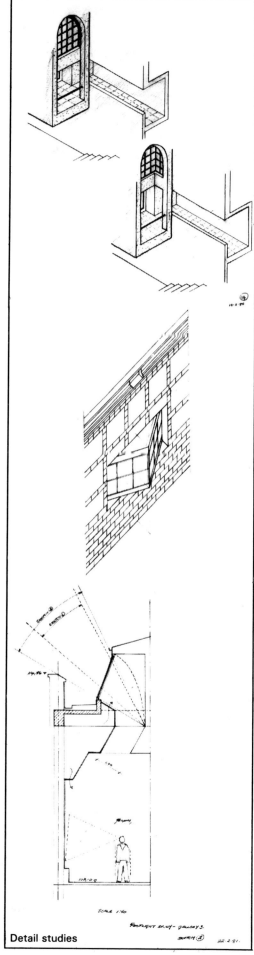

SCALE 1:50

ROOFLIGHT STUDY — GALLERY 5.

SKETCH ④   22·2·91

Detail studies

Acknowledgements

A substantial part of this publication has appeared in *Architectural Design* magazine numbers 9-10 1977, 8-9 1979, 7-8 1980 (Stirling Gold), 1-2 1982, and in *Architectural Design News Supplement* No.6 1981.

We would like to thank James Stirling for providing material, information and the cover drawing and Dennis Crompton for designing this *AD Profile*.

We also acknowledge the generous co-operation of the RIBA in providing facilities for tape-recording James Stirling, Norman Foster and Mark Girouard and the help of Rebecca Collins who transcribed them.

Our thanks go to those authors who have contributed articles and to their publishers for allowing them to be reproduced in this issue, as follows:

Articles by Paul Goldberger and Ada Louise Huxtable copyright © 1981 by The New York Times Company, reprinted by permission; articles by Charles Jencks and Robert Maxwell copyright © 1977, 1981, 1982 *Architectural Design*.

We are grateful to James Stirling for providing almost all of the illustrations, together with additional photographs taken by:

Brecht-Einzig Ltd.: Leicester University Engineering Building; Cambridge University History Building (exterior); Queens College, Oxford; Runcorn New Town Housing; Olivetti Training School, Hazlemere.

John Donat: the models of Siemens AG, Munich; Arts Centre, St Andrews University; Wallraf-Richartz Museum, Cologne; Staatsgalerie, Stuttgart; Bayer AG PF Zentrum, Monheim; Science Centre, Berlin; Turner Gallery, London.

Norman McGrath: Cambridge History Building (interior).

Masao Arai: the portrait of James Stirling.

Richard Ball: the colour drawing of Rice University School of Architecture.

Richard Cheatle: the colour drawings of the Turner Gallery.

Dennis Crompton: West London Factory; Dulwich Art Gallery; the model of the Turner Gallery.

Paul Hester: Rice University School of Architecture existing and new buildings.

Kraufmann u. Kraufmann: Staatsgalerie, Stuttgart, Richtfest.

Rudolf Schwarz: the progress photographs, Staatsgalerie, Stuttgart.

Colin Thomas: interior of the JS/MW office, London.

The arcade, Derby Civic Centre, 1970